Adult Education
for the Church

Adult Education for the Church

The Indiana Plan

Paul Bergevin and John McKinley

THE BETHANY PRESS

ST. LOUIS, MISSOURI

TABLE OF CONTENTS

---

[1]Section B of Chapter V was written by the Reverend Dr.
Roye M. Frye. Dr. Frye was asked to write this chapter because
he knows the Indiana Plan thoroughly, he has used it extensively
and he is a devoted and experienced clergyman.

PREFACE

This book describes an educational plan for adults. Its
main emphasis is on the education of adults in religious institutions. While the psychological and educational concepts used
in this volume are applicable to most programs of adult education, it is the purpose of this particular educational plan to
try to interpret these concepts in the milieu of the church.
The authors of this book are professional adult educators. No
pretense is made that they are theologians or have any training in that area or related areas.

The fact that the authors were but little better informed
than the average layman in such formal studies, which are usually in the realm of the trained clergyman, was not disadvan-
tageous. The authors were not trying to prove that they knew
theology but rather that they could take such content material
which the church thought important for their parishioners to
know and construct around the material an educational format
suited to the unique needs of the adult learners.

The authors and several of their colleagues have done similar work in other major social institutions, e.g., mental hos-
pitals and prisons.

In 1958, a volume entitled Design for Adult Education in
the Church was written by the authors of this book. This present volume is an attempt to retain or revise the useful information presented in Design for Adult Education in the Church
and eliminate that which experience over the years has indicated is no longer useful.

This book described an idea of adult education which was
dubbed "The Indiana Plan." The Indiana Plan for religious
adult education prospered. More than 240 training institutes
for participants were held during the past 12 years and from 15
to 25 are being held each year in various parts of the country.
Every state in the union has had representation at the institutes and participants have come from eight foreign countries.

i

Over the years, new ideas were used in this Plan and changes in the educational programs took place. It was felt necessary to bring this whole idea up to date with this short book which eliminates some of the material which appeared in the original book. In addition, new materials have been added and the most useful information in the original book was retained.

The church was selected for the original study which resulted in the Indiana Plan because the church represented several important factors which the authors believed would be helpful in the development of a successful educational project: (1) the church is a large, widespread institution with a great potential for adult learning; (2) the church is concerned about humanity, and to some extent does or could counteract the destructive philosophy of almost pure materialism which has most other social institutions solidly in its grip; (3) the church has many persons in it who are interested in learning or who could be stimulated to be interested; (4) the administrative organization of some communions is such that it was not difficult to get and to keep a number of experimental groups working for several years; (5) cooperation with most of the clergy and key lay persons was possible.

Without belaboring the five points mentioned above some reference should be made to the first one, i.e., the church has a great potential for adult learning. The word "potential" was used because the church in general is not at the present time an effective educational institution. It rarely educates in the sense that it tries to bring people to its point of view through a series of intellectual explorations, of confrontations with persons having different views. The notions of education frequently found in the church by the authors seemed to be overwhelmingly those of implantation, of indoctrination. Helping adult learners to come to terms with ideas by freely expressing their views, be they "acceptable" or not, was found to be rarely tolerated. And this could be expected because the clergy, with rare exceptions, knew nothing about education or the learning problems of adults. The seminaries put out the "facts" but do not know how to put them over to the people. And since the leadership had little or no training in the problems of the adult as a learner little could be expected from the followership in that area. An interesting by-product of this defect in the clergy's professional preparation is the tendency of rather large numbers of them to try to patch the situation by attaching themselves to one or more quickie training programs which are often offered by the national headquarters and educational institutions of various kinds. Attendance is good at these one- or two-week programs which sometimes teach short cuts to the solution of educational problems. The participant often comes back from this kind of meeting full of inspiration and a kind of canned knowledge -- the "be a brain surgeon by studying in your spare time" type.

True, sometimes a few persons are persistent, energetic and flexible enough to realize some back-at-home values from these experiences. Many times this is not the case, however, partly because some of us feel that we really don't need any instruction in how to learn; that all we need is faith and to memorize the information the church puts out. Another reason people don't make full use of some short-term training programs is that they are not prepared intellectually or emotionally for the experiences which take place in some of these programs which try to put as much emphasis on the learner as on the subject.

Short term training programs can help but they cannot substitute for professionally trained leadership. Clergymen need seminary training appropriate to the problems they will encounter in the field. Lay people as well as clergymen who are assigned to educational directorships in local, state, and national church offices need training in the area in which they are operating. If it is adult education, they should be trained in adult education. The adult learner in the local parish can get a great deal more from being helped by professionally trained educators than he can by listening to sermons and Bible stories which he cannot intelligently interpret in terms of his own life.

The authors have frequently stated that "The Indiana Plan" is a plan to end "plans." It is hoped that persons who participate in this kind of instruction use the ideas they get as a point of departure from which they will develop their own programs of adult learning suited to the specific and revealed needs of those participating and within the abilities of the trained leadership to handle.

No effort has ever been made to have the persons who participate in Indiana Plan Institutes call the work they do at home the "Indiana Plan." This kind of credit has not been asked for because the major thrust of this adult educational activity has been to help participants through educational means to learn to improve their understanding of God's will and the part they must play to implement this. Since we all have a provincial streak in us it is better to use every opportunity we have to emphasize the positive aspects of the program rather than having people direct some of their energy toward wondering why they are in a program called "The Indiana Plan" in Oklahoma City. And, too, it is better from the start to <u>make</u> <u>adaptations</u> <u>to</u> <u>fit</u> <u>local</u> <u>situations</u>, and to continually readjust and revise, based on solid evidence secured through evaluation. A unique feature of this Plan is that with little effort it can be adapted to specific needs of persons in different churches and different communions.

From the start the authors held some basic beliefs about the adult as a learner and about adult learning in the church. We believed that programs should be designed to provide the best possible <u>learning</u> situations; emphasis, therefore, was placed on both learning and teaching. This meant we had to start with people rather than with subject materials. And since we adults must use our new learning largely through our relationships with other persons, important emphasis was put on providing opportunities for participants to <u>use</u> part of their new learning <u>in the learning situation</u> -- with and for others. We, as learners, understand Christian teachings in terms of <u>personal</u> <u>meaning</u>

and the program came to be a means of translating Christian learning into personal action.

Another major idea which had to be taken into account in the program was the unique nature of each individual learner, who at the same time was part of the corporate body of the church. The program became both person-centered and group-centered. We are at our best as learners when we are doing what we are able and like to do as individuals and as a body of individuals. Thus a learning program based on the educational teamwork of all persons involved in the learning process seemed to be needed. The clergyman, the teachers, the leaders, and every other participant -- all -- were conceived as learners, as a team embarked on the same learning adventure.

Work of this kind is a product of many experiences which are interpreted and encouraged by numerous persons who deserve recognition. The Lilly Endowment, Inc. has repeatedly given us encouragement and financial help and we appreciate both. And the following persons have helped us over many years by giving us their critical views of our work: Mrs. Patricia Barbier, The Rev. Kenneth Barringer, Mr. J. Albert Clark, Dr. H. Walton Connelly, Mrs. Cecilia Daniel, The Rev. Canon Rudolph Devik, The Rev. Dr. Roye M. Frye, Dr. George K. Gordon, The Rev. Benton Hanon, The Rev. J. Walter Lantz, The Rev. Tom McKennell, The Rev. David Noreen, The Rev. Dr. Earl Shay, The Rev. George Oliver Taylor, The Rev. Alfred Vail. We are indebted to the persons named above and use this opportunity to formally acknowledge it.

P.B.
J.M.

CHAPTER I

ADULT RELIGIOUS EDUCATION: A PROBLEM AND A NEED

A prime educational purpose of the Church is to help us to know
God better so that we may better serve Him. But many of the
organized adult learning programs in local churches fall far
short of this goal.

There are many reasons why adults have difficulty in learning and in practicing what they know. However, there seemed to
be little virtue in pointing out educational ills in existing
programs unless good reasons could be given for pointing them
out and tested remedies provided to put in their place. So the
authors chose what was considered a positive approach to the
problem: they set out to develop an educational pattern in
which adults could learn creatively. This meant that actual
programs had to be organized and observed in operation. Only
in this way was it possible to identify some principles which
undergird a successful program and also factors which cause adult
church programs to fall short of carrying out an educational purpose of the Church.

The project began with an educational idea: that people
can learn together creatively if they will accept the responsibilities of attacking their mutual learning problems cooperatively
in an atmosphere of freedom and acceptance. Three years later,
having guided and observed experimental adult programs in 35
churches, the authors had learned how this educational idea
could be applied to develop a broad educational program.

The framework of training, study and action which brings
about this development is fairly flexible and seems to be generally applicable if it is adapted carefully to the local church.
It has been dubbed "The Indiana Plan for Adult Religious Education" and is briefly described in Chapter III.

Analyzing the past failures and successes of the project,
and the existing programs which were observed in churches of

various communions, made it possible to identify some of the significant factors which, from an educational viewpoint, combine to cause the problem of non-productive learning in adult church programs. Presented here are these significant factors which create this problem as the investigators saw the problem emerge. They are the same factors which the investigators found themselves trying to overcome.

The attempt to distinguish them here is mainly for the purpose of clarification. Actually they can neither be isolated as independent entities nor dealt with independently in practice, because each one has bearing on all the others.

A. INADEQUATE UNDERSTANDING OF THE ADULT AS LEARNER

Administrators, and adult learners too, have not understood how adult learning differs from childhood learning. This misunderstanding is perhaps the overarching reason for the existence of the other related problems which we present in this chapter. It also helps explain why many adult church programs are, in effect, extensions of the Sunday School program, using the same educational structure which has been found effective with young people.

Sunday School programs frequently use a type of formalized learning program to which youngsters are regularly exposed in their daily school life. This has been found effective largely because children haven't lived long and have had few practical opportunities to test ideas; their experience is limited. Hence a rather natural teacher-learner relationship, the child being dependent upon someone who he thinks knows the facts. The child often knows he doesn't know, and he tends to accept.

As a person grows into adulthood, however, his feeling of dependency decreases and he begins to think he knows. He resists reorganizing his attitudes and behaviors which have grown out of his response to many years of experience. Especially does the adult resist someone else's attempt to force him to reorganize himself. The teacher-pupil relationship in adult groups, therefore, must be considerably modified if the program

2

is to be most successful. Mainly it is a problem of recognizing that adults are both dependent and independent. Extremes are dangerous. It takes more than simply telling in order to help an adult who has cherished some misconceptions for decades. He does not usually make rapid adjustments. If creative learning is to occur, <u>adult learners must be treated differently than the children</u> in the usual Sunday School class.

The fact is, adult learning is a highly personal thing and we sometimes fail to consider it as personal. "Certainly," we say, "we all know that each learner is unique; that's an idea as old as the hills." Why, then, haven't we based our adult programs on this idea? Why have we relied so heavily on mass methods of exposing learners to religious information? And why is the amount of time we spend on a given subject in our classes so regulated by artificial time-spans? We level off people and we try to measure by the clock, instead of by our needs, the amount of time we give to a unit in a curriculum. If adult learning is personal, why not begin with persons and base our programs on principles that make for effective personal adult learning?

First of all, it is when we become actively involved as persons in the learning process that we have the best chance to make learning personal. When we are treated as "soaker-uppers" of factual information, or as human sponges, we have no chance to become actively involved as persons.

Secondly, if we are to learn most effectively, we adults must ourselves discover and recognize a personal reason for learning about a given topic. It is not enough for someone to tell us why he thinks it is important for us to learn a certain thing. Learning programs should begin and deal with needs which learners recognize as needs. This condition can be met most satisfactorily when we learners become actively involved in some way in planning and evaluating the educational experience.

Third, we adults must share the responsibility for the success of the learning experience. We can best become responsible for our learning if we actively participate in some way. There is no short cut; it is not enough to be told that we are responsible. We must _experience_ what it means to accept responsibility for the growth of ourselves and others in our educational ventures.

Some Suggestions About the Adult as a Learner

A great deal of teaching and leading discussions and carrying on adult education work in general is done by persons who are not professional teachers or trained adult educators. Most persons occupied in volunteer educational activities have had little or no training in how to teach or in the nature of the learner (the person they are trying to teach). The notion held by some of us is that if you know a subject well enough, or if you are keenly interested in helping others, or preferably both, you can effectively teach. While interest is a potent motivating factor in quality teaching and knowledge of the subject is essential, these factors alone cannot accomplish as much as is possible for the time and effort spent. Training is necessary. Some understanding of how to teach or lead discussions and some knowledge of the learner is vital to the successful transferal of information and ideas.

Since an extensive training program is not possible for the great numbers of volunteer leaders and teachers, some short but reasonably effective training programs have been developed to bring the leader or teacher into a productive relationship with the adult learner by translating and interpreting content and transmitting information. And, of course, a good leader or a good teacher is skilled in helping the learners to translate, interpret, and transmit ideas and information to each other. A good leader or teacher knows how to put a goodly share of the responsibility of the teaching-learning transaction on the learner himself.

4

The Indiana Plan Institute is an attempt to help train non-professional, volunteer leaders in the art of developing appropriate programs in adult education and in conducting such programs. A vital part of the function of every participant who acts as a leader is to know something about the learner. Too often all learners are treated as if they had the same needs and abilities, and the idea seems to be that if you hammer at them long enough, being sure to smile now and then, things will happen. True, things happen, but not always what was expected.

The more we can know about those who learn, including ourselves as learners, the more we can help them to make each learning experience a fruitful adventure. More work has been done in studying the child as a learner, and much more is known than is used. Following are a few suggestions which may prove to be helpful, if used.

An adult is not a grown-up child. He differs significantly in some respects. The following brief statements might help us to understand the nature of the adult learner particularly, and thereby suggest programs of learning which would be effective. These points are taken from the book A Philosophy for Adult Education (Seabury Press):

1. Adults come to learning programs with a more definite "set" than children;

2. Adult personality is more permanently fixed for good or ill;

3. Adults have more emotional connections with words, situations, institutions, and people than do children;

4. Many learners bring negative feelings with them to the learning situation because they resent authority;

5. Adults are more under the burden of certain stereotypes like personality and belief than are children, who are in a more formative stage of development;

6. Inadequacy and failure is more likely to be in the forefront of an adult's mind than of a child's;

7. The adult may see new learning as more of a threat to the balance and integration he has attempted to achieve;

8. Most adults must rather quickly see more relevance and immediacy of application than children do;

9. A group of, say, fifteen adults will usually have more
    variations in skills, interests, experiences, and ed-
    ucation than a similar group of children. They might
    be considered more highly differentiated;

10. Adult attitudes are difficult to change. If learning
    is not shaped to fit a real or symptomatic need, the
    change often will be forgotten or rejected;

Some additional problems which sometimes concern the adult
learner and his learning productivity follow:

1. Worry over his health

2. A sense of inadequacy

3. Difficulty in adjusting to new ideas or conditions

4. Harking back to the past

5. Less activity, a tendency to stay at home

6. Loneliness

In addition to these points there are physiological factors
that need to be considered by the person responsible for adult
learning programs. Many of these factors are known to most
people but like some things we know we don't do much about
them, and in this case it reacts to the detriment of the adult
learner. Factors which, if considered, would make quite a
difference in an adult learning program are listed below:

-Many adults do not hear well or they don't hear as well
as they did as youngsters. Some adults will try to cover
up this deficiency.

-Adult vision decreases with age. This is particularly
noticeable in older age groups.

-An adult's circulation is often not what it used to be.
They get cold.

-Many older adults are unable to climb stairs.

-A general degeneration of the nervous system occurs with
age increase which can not only impair vision and hearing but affects an older adult learner's memory and
attention span.

-Often older adults don't feel very well and this can
affect the way they react to situations arising in the
learning group.

Being aware of these factors of the aging learner can help
the volunteer adult educator to develop programs of learning

6

that fit the need of the learner. We can, for example, be more careful to have comfortable, well-lighted, warm, quiet rooms for the sessions. We can talk clearly and loudly and slowly. We can be friendly, pleasant, cooperative. We can smile a lot and put appropriate humor to work. We can show exceptional patience and take the whole affair in an easy going, informal manner. Older adults do not adapt to stress as well as young people. We can make every effort to encourage, compliment and involve the learner. If we don't accomplish what we set out to do, we don't show concern; we don't push the learner but rather try to bring him to the new facts or ideas in a relaxed atmosphere. We maintain quality, but quality can be achieved without seriously disturbing the learner. And if you disturb the volunteer learner too much you won't have a program at all. He won't come back.

Different persons who are volunteer adult educators operate in different ways. And this is as it should be. But if the few points mentioned above are given thoughtful consideration and used constructively according to the ability of each leader the quality of volunteer adult educational programs will show marked improvement.

The adult at any age can learn, but there is a gradual decline in learning ability as the learner becomes older. **In general this decline is not as significant** as many persons have believed. Two factors are, however, of great significance: the attitude that the adult learner, himself, has toward learning, and the quality of the adult learning program in which he is involved.

B. TIMIDITY AND FEAR

Many adults who attend and take part in church learning activities wish only to sit and listen. Some of this passiveness may no doubt be attributed to lethargy and lack of interest. A surprising number of persons, however, wish desperately to explore some of the learning problems they have in the area of religious

7

education but are afraid to suggest what these problems are, and are fearful of dealing with them.

One of the problems that we must overcome is the fear we have of each other and the clergyman. We fear to let others know how little we know about religion and life. Some adults like to think of themselves as beyond the age of learning. We may know we don't have many of the answers, but we act as though we do because we are expected to act that way. We fear acting otherwise. We fear to reveal our ignorance to the clergyman. We fear open disagreement in church learning activities. And yet we often wish that more of our programs would deal with the realities and problems of Christian living. Helping participants to overcome this fear and to develop freedom of expression is one of the first problems that must be solved in the development of an effective co-operative adult program. Without freedom of expression (a) we cannot adequately reveal our learning needs, (b) we cannot help each other as responsible members of a learning team, (c) we cannot openly identify the obstacles to our understanding, (d) we cannot honestly evaluate our church programs and activities.

Many of us apparently believe that it is bad for us to "say out loud" ideas that may be wrong or that we can express but poorly. Do we hug them close rather than risk letting our friends learn we are ignorant? Or do we try to fool ourselves and God by keeping quiet or by saying "the right words" without knowing what they mean to us?

Some few of us are overwhelmed by the information and knowledge we don't have; thus we convince ourselves that we have no right to an opinion, especially when the clergyman is present. ("He spent many years studying religion!") True, he has spent **years** studying **religion**: he still **has** only a part of the educational formula, **and** some **clergymen** have little or no knowledge of educational procedures that make **religion** meaningful to people. He can help us, but he can't do it for us. Each of us also has a vital part of the formula -- our own minds, feelings, and experience which we must use to try to understand our relationship to God. In short, we had better develop some opinions and get those we have into the open. Many of us can profit by facing the educational task openly and together. When we do this, the clergyman is often better able to use his talents most wisely to help us.

C. TRAINING FOR LEADERSHIP ONLY

Much emphasis has been placed on the training of lay leaders in the church, and this training has not been in vain. Lay leaders will always be needed. Indeed, many church programs are held together mainly by those dedicated persons who have been willing to accept the responsibilities of leadership. And it is this very fact that raises the question: is it enough to train only leaders?

When leaders are trained to accept the major or whole responsibility for the success of a program or an activity, those who are led often become mere followers. They are quite willing to be dependent upon their leaders. For example, the teacher of the adult class is too often forced to assume the full responsibility for the teaching-learning process. Participants expect him not only to teach them but to "learn them" (learn for them). Part of this difficulty lies in the fact that we learners do not know how to participate responsibly. We therefore cannot accept the responsibility for actively helping ourselves, our fellow learners, and our leaders in a joint enterprise. We need to learn how to work with each other in the educational process. We must become aware of actual ways in which we can help each other and our leaders. Then our leaders must give us opportunities to practice our skills and share in the educational process.

Unfortunately, too many leaders of adult groups are leading because of a need they personally have. They need to be in charge, to be the boss. They find it difficult to participate as one of the group unless the whole group looks to them

9

for direction. These leaders are preventing the participants from maturing, from getting the greatest possible benefit from the corporate learning experience, because these leaders are giving the people what these leaders think they need without involving the other participants in this great process of co-operative discovery.

Training in the skills and duties of responsible participation is not a daring new concept; it is an ever-present need dictated by common sense. A team functions best when all its members know how to work together. Our athletic coaches have known this fact for years. They don't give their team captains special training and assume that the rest of the team will function smoothly. The whole team practices together, and every member is responsible for helping accomplish the final aim. It should be so in adult religious education. Training leaders is a step in the right direction, but that alone is not effective. Few short cuts are.

D. PRESCRIBED NEEDS AND EXTREMELY CENTRALIZED PLANNING

Many adults refuse to do anything for themselves in religious education. Usually they do not know how, and too often they are fearful and have not been given an opportunity to do so. So they insist that someone -- preferably an expert -- do it for them. Clergymen and other professional church educators have often felt that they must deal with this situation by doing as much as they can educationally _for_ people. But frequently this effort has led them to try to do too much for the learners. As a result: (1) clergymen may try to reach too many people too rapidly with too much -- or with information that is perceived by the learners as inappropriate; (2) one person, or a very small group, plans educational programs without knowing the needs which the learners recognize as needs; (3) facts are presented to learners before they are ready to try to understand those facts; (4) too few opportunities are provided for helping people to relate information to their experience.

These short cuts are inadequate for several reasons. First, the brief, highly concentrated doses of education frequently result in the use of much jargon, such as theological or psychological language which many teachers and learners do not take time to translate into personal meaning. Secondly, although time is "saved" when only one or a very few people do the planning, the learners do not feel sufficiently responsible for the success of the program as a personal learning venture. It is not _of_ them but for them.

Thirdly, since we adults are timid about mentioning our needs in adult religious education and often have not recognized what our real needs and learning problems are, it is not enough simply to ask us what kind of programs would be of interest. This is a first step, but the solution is not that simple. We adult learners must have opportunities to sincerely discover our own actual needs over a period of time, if we are expected to do much about filling them. We can be led to recognize some of them, but we must make the recognition; no one else can do it wholly for us. How can we do it? Here is one way:

First we need to develop freedom of expression and to learn how to work together as responsible members of a learning team. Then we can begin with what we _think_ our needs are, because these we can most readily understand and accept. Finally, over a period of time, we can learn to recognize some of our deeper religious educational needs and accept some responsibility for planning and conducting programs that help fill those needs. We learn after we develop the readiness to learn. If we all share responsibility for the success of the programs, we can forthrightly evaluate the outcomes and adjust future programs and activities to the purpose of the church and to those needs of ours which relate to that purpose.

We often become slaves of subject materials because we begin with them instead of with people. Repeatedly people are forced to fit into subject matter rather than using appropriate subject matter to fit the needs of a particular group at a particular time. The local planners should use the resources that will best help learners meet the needs which they recognize. These needs are prior to materials, and the highest authority for discovering these needs is the learners themselves.

E. GOALS SELDOM UNDERSTOOD IN CONCRETE TERMS BY LEARNERS AND SELDOM USED BY PLANNERS

A major goal of religious education is simply to learn how better to relate ourselves to God so that we can serve Him better. One of the most serious causes of failure in programs of adult religious education lies in the inability (and hesitancy) of planners and other participants to identify this goal in at least tentative specific terms and to develop programs that help them to meet the goal in specific ways.

To many of us it comes as a shock to learn that we are expected to change as a result of religious educational programs. We agree that we should learn to know God better and to serve Him. And yet we often hesitate to translate this ultimate goal into more specific goals or desirable outcomes that will give practical direction to our learning programs. We especially avoid stating such goals openly; it is too much like setting out deliberately to change ourselves. And yet that is exactly what we are expected to help each other to do, with God's help.

> "We should not look too closely at specific reasons why we attend a religious educational program. That makes it mechanical, when actually religious education is a very personal thing. We should take what we can and not worry about goals. We all know more or less why we're here. Besides, it is embarrassing to come right out and say what we're trying to learn and why."

Although seldom voiced in precisely these terms, this kind of thinking seems to have helped keep adult religious education out on the edge of our lives where it takes its place among other activities that call forth little effort and cause a correspondingly little change in our behavior. Even a few administrators seem to consider it unnecessary to talk openly about specific goals of religious education. These attitudes help prevent our growth, for the basic goal of adult religious education will remain an intangible objective if it is not brought into the framework of reality that is recognized by the participants.

The educational goals of church organizations, if any, are sometimes buried in a book of by-laws where they remain classically formal and comprehensive -- too general to be of use to learners or planners. While many of the various study groups, church organizations, and programs do have clear, specific goals, these goals are sometimes not sufficiently related to a major educational goal of the church: growth in understanding of our relationship with God. In short, too many activities and educational efforts seem to be ends in themselves rather than means. Careful examination will often reveal that the leaders of church programs and organizations do not have a clear view of the goals their enterprise is supposed to accomplish. Over a long period of time such programs often result in either busy-work or shallow talk.

The need is great for opportunities in which we can learn to establish and share clear, specific goals that can be used to guide educational programs and activities. Whatever goals are used must be constantly examined and frequently advanced as we make progress, but at any one point in the process, we must either see or think we see the reason why we are engaged.

F. TOKEN EVALUATION, MADE BY PLANNERS ONLY
The problem of evaluating religious educational programs and activities is not recognized as a problem by many people. We avoid examining our goals often by assuming that everyone knows why he attends an educational meeting. We often avoid evaluating activities and programs (1) by assuming that people automatically incorporate the new learning into their lives, and (2) by assuming that the programs could not be improved upon very much even if they were evaluated. Those assumptions are

good ways to help us dodge the issue, but they are not the only reasons why evaluation has been consistently avoided.

Why have we avoided appraising openly how effective our church learning experiences are, and determining how they might be made more effective? There seem to be several reasons.

Too often all evaluation is a mental labeling of "good" or "bad" by one person, or by those who manage or have planned the program. It is the learner's evaluation that is most important in any area of voluntary adult education. He alone can say whether an educational program or activity has meaning for him and what meaning it has for him. Both learners and administrators need to take part cooperatively in periodic organized evaluation if evaluation is to serve a useful purpose in improving programs.

Another reason why effective evaluation by all people concerned has been virtually impossible in the church: participants have not understood the main purpose of church programs. This purpose has not been reduced to specific goals they can identify in the various programs and activities. Unless we know what we set out to do we cannot begin to determine whether our activities are helping us to do it. Again we see the need for clear goals constantly examined. If we don't know where we are going we certainly wouldn't be able to recognize whether or not we got there.

One reason why even simple evaluation procedures (getting learner's reactions to a program) have seldom been used in the church is that many administrators and program chairmen apparently haven't thought of giving participants the responsibility of evaluating. Doubtless it might prove embarrassing in cases in which only one or two persons planned the program. We can safely evaluate a joint effort but we hesitate "to look a gift horse in the mouth." This situation points to the need of broadening the base of responsibility and involving more persons in the planning of programs and activities.

Needs prescribed by upper levels of administration are not always recognized as needs by the learners. And to evaluate programs planned by administrators alone would appear to be questioning the wisdom of the experts. Thus it is perhaps not unusual for both the learners and the administrators to resist evaluating these programs.

Another obstacle to open, organized evaluation is the idea that everything relating to a church is highly personal and hush-hush, including our opinions on the results and methods of our educational experiences. It is true that we learn and grow in our understanding of God as individual persons. Many aspects of our growth cannot be and should not be translated into results we can number and reel off as items on a list. Much of our learning is too personal to share exactly as we feel or know it. Nevertheless, when we learn together as persons, as one of many members of that one body with shared goals, we must occasionally see whether we are moving toward the main goal and how we might better approach it. In order to do this we must evaluate to the extent that we are able and willing.

Some administrators assume that most learners aren't capable of judging the worth of a program. ("They don't know a _good_ sermon when they hear one.") But programs are _good_ only to the extent which they meet the needs of the particular learners involved. The polished sermon that might rate an "A" when delivered at a seminary is a poor educational experience for the listeners in a local church if they can see no personal meaning in it. The learners themselves hold the keys to evaluation in adult religious education.

To overcome these obstacles to evaluate, we need to develop freedom of expression, clear goals, and evaluation procedures. And we all need to assume a share of the responsibility for planning, conducting and evaluating programs.

15

G. PREOCCUPATION WITH SUBJECT MATTER

Obviously subject matter is essential and important. A body of facts, however, is of greatest educational value only as learners use it as a means of achieving desirable growth. Subject matter itself should not become the end, sought for its own sake.

In many of our church learning activities, we have set out deliberately to learn more about the Bible merely for the purpose of knowing more about the Bible. The problem becomes acute when we begin to think of "the facts" as the beginning and the end of religious education. When this happens, we gear our programs to the subject matter instead of to the learners. This situation generates these kinds of problems:

1. we attempt to "cover" a certain amount of material in a definite time span;

2. we become annoyed when learners bring up something that might throw us off schedule or that seems to us indirectly related to the subject at hand;

3. we force-feed the facts in an attempt to fit the individual to the curriculum;

4. our meetings bog down in definitions and theological intricacies;

5. learners must often be satisfied with pat, standardized solutions to life problems and with religious information which remains unrelated to their lives.

Church educators must finally recognize that religious education is more than exposing people to a body of subject matter. Subject matter or content is one resource, and an important one. But there must be a balance between content (what is communicated and learned) and process (how persons communicate and learn) if the learning experience is to be most fruitful. We cannot afford to overlook the educative value of people's active participation, feelings, and inter-relationships. We cannot afford to dismiss the variety of group procedures by which adults are known to learn effectively. These procedures are part of process, which is -- like subject matter (content) -- a means to effective learning. Subject matter is only as vital to the learner as its vehicle, process, permits it to be. The

16

way we feel as we learn, and the way we go about learning, affect how much we learn and what we learn.

We tend to the extremes -- either toward content or toward process -- in our religious education. For example, a stranger once attended a church service and heard an excellent sermon on the brotherhood of man. The point was well made that we are all related as children of God. But when the sermon ended the stranger left the church as a stranger. Nobody even nodded to him. He had had an educational experience that emphasized content. There was process, but it did not reinforce the content. On the other side of the ledger are the church experiences that are almost entirely on the process level -- fellowship meetings, for example. There is content of a sort (a variety of things are talked about), but they are often surface matters. These meetings have a purpose, but we don't look beneath the surface in order to make the most of our group life as a resource. And yet, our life together is the arena where we are expected to interpret through our actions the content of religious teachings.

If our relationships with others in the learning setting, our feelings, our experiences, are important -- if they help determine how and what we learn, we should take them into account and harness them along with subject matter when we plan our educational programs.

H. INADEQUATE EDUCATIONAL PROCEDURES

The sermon, the lecture, the book review and the adult Sunday School class are important media of adult education in the Church. But these alone seldom combine into a well-rounded, effective program.

The possibility that these activities, through constant repetition, may fall into a dull pattern through mere lack of variety is not the only reason why they are insufficient. The fact is, our choice of educational procedures should be determined by (a) our goals, (b) our resources, (c) the nature of

17

the topic, and (d) the experiences and __needs__ of the participants. Obviously we should not arbitrarily fit every program
into the same mold. Yet we tend to. Take, for instance, the
token 30-minute programs (perhaps a book report or a lecture)
conducted once a month by some church organizations. Many of
these are excellent presentations, but endless presentations
do not allow people to come to grips with what is presented.
As a matter of fact, such repetitive programs which really do
not involve the listener tend to establish methodological
habits that future program chairmen hesitate to violate.

The sermon and the lecture, for example, are two ways
which sometimes inspire people and present information. But
people cannot fill all their religious educational needs by
listening to sermons or lectures. It is not sufficient merely
to articulate truths in the presence of learners. Most adults
need opportunities to actively explore, digest, and assimilate
what is presented. Different procedures are required to provide
the kinds of programs that are dictated by different needs.

Program administrators are often unable to fit appropriate
procedures to the various educational tasks at hand. A few of
them are openly scornful of using combinations of various educational procedures. Some of them seem to resist changing
traditional patterns for fear of appearing not to trust God
implicitly to handle the whole educational process. Many of
them resist using procedures appropriate to adult learning for
reasons such as (a) effective procedures frequently involve the
learners actively in the learning process, and such activities
are threatening to teachers or leaders who are accustomed to
proclaiming the truth, and (b) they simply have not been taught
how to select and use a variety of appropriate procedures.

The question is not whether we should taint religious education with a variety of secular educational procedures for the
sake of achieving variety. Rather, the question is: Why should
we not adapt the best known educational procedures to the unique

problems and needs of religious education for the purpose of making adult learning more productive in the church?

SUMMARY

THE PROBLEM	THE NEED
1. Inadequate understanding of the adult as learner	1. Opportunities for lay and clergy to understand better the problems and principles of adult learning
2. Timidity and fear	2. Freedom of expression
3. Training for leadership only	3. Training in both leadership and other kinds of responsible participation

4. Needs prescribed by authorities:
  a. Extremely centralized planning
  b. Jargon, unrelated information
	4. Beginning with needs learners recognize
	  a. Let participants help determine the program
	  b. Have opportunities for learners to relate information to experience

5. Goals **seldom determined** or **understood** by participants and seldom used by planners	5. Clear, shared goals which planners use to give direction to programs
6. Token evaluation, made by planners only	6. Organized evaluation by all participants
7. Preoccupation with subject matter	7. Balance between content and process
8. Use of inadequate educational procedures	8. Training in the use of appropriate procedures

CHAPTER II

EDUCATIONAL CONDITIONS OF
THE INDIANA PLAN

We are able to make the best use of our corporate learning opportunities when certain conditions exist. These conditions concern not only the physical environment in which we learn, but also the emotional environment, the manner in which we are involved in the learning process, and the extent and nature of our participation in it. In the Indiana Plan for Adult Religious Education these conditions are expressed as:

    A. Training for the Learning Team

    B. Freedom of Expression

    C. Active Individual Participation

    D. Sharing in Program Development

    E. Voluntary Learning Activities

    F. Formal and Informal Educational Procedures

    G. Outward Growth

The seven sections of this chapter explain the significance of these conditions and how they operate as the Indiana Plan.

SECTION A

TRAINING FOR THE LEARNING TEAM

1. The Learning Team

The Indiana Plan for Adult Religious Education starts in a church with the training of one or more groups of usually 12 to 15 persons each. Each group is trained to become a learning team. As the Plan is implemented, more and more learning teams are trained, and the original learning teams eventually become nuclei for an expanding program composed of a variety of educational activities.[1] The final training objective of the Plan

---

[1] Other activities are described in Chapter III.

is to continue expanding through learning teams until the whole congregation becomes involved in both training and other related educational activities.

2. The Participants

Each person trained in a learning team is a participant. But participants play different roles in the learning venture. There are five ways participants can take part on the learning team. To differentiate these five roles the following titles have been assigned: (a) the group participant, (b) the leader, (c) the resource person, (d) the observer, and (e) the trainer. Each one of these participants plays a specific role on the team.

a. The Group Participant. A group participant is a member of the learning team who takes an active part in the educational process as one of the learners in the group. There are, of course, more group participants than any other members of the team. They are not exclusively the learners, however, because in this Plan all participants are learners. Group participants might be roughly compared with the students in a formal educational situation. Their duties and responsibilities, however, far exceed those of the average student in a formal class.

When the learning program develops as it should, each one of us uses his own talents and expresses himself in some constructive manner. A trained group participant:

(1) shares his ideas, opinions and insights with others.

(2) helps others to say what they are trying to say.

(3) acts as a good listener.

(4) helps the leader in smoothing over rough spots and tense situations, keeping on the topic, and helping control the leader if necessary.

(5) offers to accept responsibility for (a) helping select resource materials, (b) securing resource persons or acting as one, if called upon, (c) helping make physical arrangements and doing other jobs necessary for successful programs, (d) taking his turn as leader, (e) serving as observer.

(6) volunteers to serve on necessary committees.

(7) reads and studies assigned and related resource materials prior to the meetings, comes prepared to offer more than his opinion.

One who willingly assumes a share of the work necessary for a successful educational adventure is a productive group participant. He is learning to be a responsible co-learner and at the same time to deal with subject matter. He is learning by talking, by listening, by reading, by planning and by evaluating; in other words, by actively doing something creative along with his fellow learners.

b. The Leader. A leader is a participant who volunteers temporarily to perform certain duties with the learning team. The leader aids members of the learning team to learn together. He does not impart facts to the group participants on the topic being discussed, but rather helps them to discover the personal significance of the facts. The leader's role is different for each different educational procedure used by the learning team. He acts as a discussion leader when the team uses group discussion. In this capacity he acts as a stimulator, guide, helper. He helps others express themselves instead of offering his own ideas. He will have a chance to express himself as a group participant when he again becomes a group participant.

The leader may act as a moderator during the use of such procedures as forums, panels and colloquies, when the learning team expands and various educational methods are indicated.

In the conventional classroom, where the learner-leader roles are sharply divided, the learner waits for the leader to lay out the course and direct the progress of the group. In this Plan, however, the leader is as much a learner as any person in the program. He and everyone in the program knows it.

All participants are given the same kind of training in the skills and responsibilities of both discussion leadership and group participation. Those of us who would lead must also learn to be group participants. More than half of the participants (6 out of 10 persons) trained in the initial procedures

22

eventually assume voluntarily the role of leader in some part of the program. Even those who do not wish to volunteer for the leader's job know the problems of leadership and are therefore better group participants. Actually these non-leaders perform a certain part of the leader's role. The group participant helps the leader do his job. The leader may call the signals but everyone knows the game and checks the signals.

Many persons have led people toward immaturity by making them dependent. In this type of learning, where we are to some degree struggling against ourselves, we are well occupied; we should not have to struggle against a domineering leader, too. Although the word we use is "leader," the implication here is that he helps to lead toward growth and maturity in himself as well as others by using knowledge and procedures which promote these ends. When we are trained in this kind of leadership, we learn to talk no more than is necessary, to help the group participants to accept responsibility and to learn to deal with their problems by themselves.

In the Indiana Plan for Adult Religious Education, an increasing number of people are equipped to take their turn at the helm because:

(1) All participants (which includes future leaders) are given basic training in both leadership and group participation. We all learn leadership, not by a short course in techniques alone, but also by continuous practice as leaders and group participants in real learning situations.

(2) We learn what effective participation is and what our specific responsibilities are in this basic training; we make it meaningful by learning through concrete experience in real learning situations.

(3) Leadership is constantly changed. Everyone has a chance to serve as a leader or co-leader if he wants to. (Two persons working together as leaders often help guide the group more effectively than a single leader can.)

Since this educational plan emphasizes learning how to share, assuming personal responsibility and using existing resources, a large number of persons must assume leadership responsibilities if we are to make the most of our resources. Some of us have certain talents and personality traits which, when combined with adequate training and practice, make us good leaders. Others do not have the same combination of traits which make them effective leaders. These differences are clear to even a casual observer in any situation where we gather to work, worship, or study together. Some of us can't be effective leaders, some of us can, and some of us don't want to be. There are many potential leaders, however, who can be encouraged and trained. And some of these persons will be revealed through such a program as this.

Some few of us never volunteer for the leadership role but we also know about leadership responsibilities because we were trained with everyone else in the group. Therefore, we can share responsibility for part of the leadership even though we take part as a group participant. No one puts the whole responsibility on the leader, for he is only a helper and a guide. He's in the same boat as every other person in the group: each one of us as a participant (not the leader alone) is responsible for the success or failure of the whole program.

c. The Resource Person. A member of the learning team who has a special fund of knowledge which is needed to support a part of the educational program is called the resource person. A resource person is qualified to speak with some authority on a particular subject. Usually he is a person from outside the group who is asked to attend the learning program on certain occasions and supply information that would assist the participants in dealing with a particular topic.

In selecting a resource person, members of the learning team would ask themselves several questions. Why do we need a resource person at this point? Specifically what do we want him to do? How long will we need him? Both the members of the learning team and the person who is to act as resource person must know the answers to these questions if this part of the program is to be conducted successfully. We obtain the services of a resource person to do a specific job at a specific time.

The talents of the resource person may be used by the learners in various ways. He sits with the group, if it is a discussion group, and listens to their remarks. Periodically members of the learning team direct specific questions to him and he is expected to give definite answers. His role is information-giver, but not speech maker. He does not prepare to present a fixed body of information for the occasion. He fits in as an integral part of the continuing discussion when needed. In such adult educational media as the symposium, the speech-forum, the panel, and panel-forum, the resource person prepares in advance to present appropriate remarks.

d. The Observer. An observer is an important member of the learning team. He plays the ears and eyes of an educational team too busy with what is going on to pay much attention to how it is going. By standing aside and fixing his attention on one specific aspect of the learning venture -- how we actually carry on -- the observer can be a vital spoke in our corporate learning wheel. Like the leader, the observer is a regular member of the group who has volunteered to perform, for a meeting or two, a specific task for the team. The volunteer observer's job should be passed around so all may have an opportunity to enrich their learning experiences through serving in this role.

The observer sits quietly during the meeting and records what is happening. His job is restricted to observing the process -- the forces at work which seem to help or hinder productive learning in group situations. The observer, then, sits with the group but does not take part orally in the discussion. He participates by observing and recording information which will help the learning team to become more proficient as an educational unit and by reporting his observations when asked.

Such observations are included as:

(1) Are we sticking to the point? If not, why?

(2) Is the group participation fairly well-balanced?

(3) Are we taking our share of the load as group participants or do we depend too much on the leader? (Examples)

(4) How does the leader affect the group?

(5) How does the group affect the leader?

(6) Are we helping each other to express ourselves? to learn?

(7) Is there a tense or relaxed atmosphere? If so, why?

After the discussion, the observer usually reports his general observations to the group and stimulates a short evaluation called a critique. As skillfully as possible, he tries to help the group participants to analyze carefully specific problems which may have been hindering their progress in learning together. The observer can spark this evaluation with well-phrased questions, but the evaluation is a group learning effort. We try together to identify our shortcomings as co-learners so we naturally don't expect a lecture from the observer.

"Do you think we really understood at the start of this meeting what we were trying to accomplish?" "Did that argument settle the problem? What did it do?" The participants can usually solve their own process problems when helped by impersonal, objective questions, skillfully presented by the observer. And everyone can gain some vital insights by serving as observer.

During the early meetings of a training group, it is valuable to have an observer at each session. Later, when the group becomes more cohesive and begins to operate as a learning team, this role can be used less frequently.

When the program expands and procedures other than group discussion are used an observer should also be employed. The observer, in this instance, can discuss his observations with those who are designated as responsible for the meeting.

e. The Trainer. The trainer is a person qualified to teach the participants this educational Plan. The trainer may come from outside the local church, or he or she may be associated with the church. He is often a professional lay or clergy leader in religious education, but he may be a qualified non-professional lay leader who has learned how to guide the developing Plan. In any case, the trainer must be sufficiently qualified as a trainer, most persons attend an institute designed to train trainers. The institute is discussed in Chapter V.

SECTION B

FREEDOM OF EXPRESSION

1. Introduction

Freedom of expression as used in the Indiana Plan means the absence of undue restraint in telling others our thoughts and feelings. In the beginning stages of this program much effort must be exerted to combat the fears which prevent us from expressing ourselves honestly and freely. This effort to develop freedom of expression is necessary in order to establish a climate in which creative learning can flourish. Fear often causes us to say what others want to hear or what we think others expect us to say. Such fear inhibits fruitful learning, both for us and for those with whom we are learning.

Adults who voluntarily gather together to explore new ideas or to broaden their understanding of old ones usually bring a surprising amount of knowledge to the learning situation. Often this knowledge is more practical and less organized than academic learning, but it represents a valuable potential. Sometimes what adults know is beclouded with doubts and lack of self-confidence -- so much so that they **are** highly reluctant to express themselves for fear they will be laughed at or will appear "not very smart."

To promote freedom of expression, it is desirable that all co-learners become acquainted with each other. The degree of acquaintance that will insure fruitful participation requires much more effort than the usual formalities of a handshake and an introduction. Therefore, each adult must be helped and encouraged to express himself during the first few meetings of a new group of learners so that his fellow-learners may discover how he feels and what he thinks about a number of things. He must be made to feel that he can say what he honestly feels and that his right to his opinion will be accepted; that he will not be rejected as a person. At the beginning of an educational experience in which the learners are inexperienced and untrained in actively sharing and learning with others, the meetings generally produce some seemingly purposeless and superficial talk. Actually a certain amount of such talk is important. It is a necessary step in the development of freedom of expression.

2. Nature of Freedom of Expression

In terms of the topic under discussion, some personal opinions and ideas expressed in the heat of emotional involvement may seem irrelevant. But to a trained leader they are quite important, for he recognizes that effective learning cannot take place until people feel free to express the opinions they hold. Free expression serves as a cathartic and helps to bring about emotional release which in a sense opens the way for learning. When open and free expression is attained, learning is ready to begin. The fact that the expressed opinions are "right" or "wrong" at this point is not as significant as the fact that the person expressing an opinion is thereby

    a. "Loosening up" himself.

    b. Helping others to muster enough courage to talk.

    c. Giving the leader and group participants a chance to know him better.

        (1) What he thinks.

        (2) How he expresses what he thinks.

    d. Fulfilling his own need to "be somebody," a unique person.

e. Helping himself and others to recognize by verbal expression some feelings and ideas which may have been deterrents to new learning.

f. Beginning an experience which can help him become a disciplined and useful member of the learning team.

One cannot be taught to express oneself freely in the same way that a person can be taught to make a dress or learn the words to a hymn. The process of developing freedom of expression requires that each group participant be offered one opportunity and then another and another until release is realized, and the greater part of the process should be carried on by the group participants. With a moderate amount of stimulation and encouragement by the leader and fellow learners, most people will soon begin to express their opinions, whatever the subject.

Many participants know little about their church and what it teaches. Careful thinking often has been seriously hampered by the learners' fixed ideas and opinions. In the early stages many participants will defend their opinions vigorously rather than examine them. But, at this time, it is important that the leader offer all the group participants full opportunity to express themselves and continue to encourage free expression without being too much concerned about the amount of time consumed, without interrupting the talkers or trying to correct them. If a talker feels that what he says is true or that the doubts he expresses are reasonable to him, persuasion or dogmatic answers on the part of a well-intentioned clergyman or other person may have little significant effect on him. The group participant is not yet emotionally set to deal objectively with contradictory facts which some other person might present. He is engrossed with expressing what he has on his mind, and the leader must see to it that neither himself nor the group prevents the participant from doing so. This struggle on the part of the group participant is often the beginning of an attempt to make an adjustment to his fellow learners which

29

thereby prepares the way for a later productive series of learning experiences.

The overcoming of this resistance to change is a condition of growth for the adult learner. He must be given the opportunity to express himself freely in order that he may begin to recognize in himself some of the problems which inhibit his learning. Freedom of expression may give him a chance to see what he is resisting and why he does so. The progress the group is making on the question with which they are dealing, at this stage, is not as important as the discoveries which they are making about themselves, about others in the group, and about the ordinary and unique situations which transpire during the meetings. The participants are, in a sense, getting ready to learn together by sharing, listening, and talking. They are coming to know their fellow learners and to feel that they can honestly and openly expose their ignorance and their doubts without being laughed at, scorned, or talked about by the "teacher" or "important" members of their learning team.

Freedom of expression must not be reserved exclusively for the group discussion method of learning; it is valuable in many learning procedures -- at all stages through which a group evolves.

3. How to Use Freedom of Expression as an Educational Condition
As indicated before, freedom of expression must be encouraged at the beginning of the program although many of the ideas expressed will not be related to the subject being explored and may be expressed in what seems to be a rather shabby fashion. It is important, therefore, that members of the learning team begin as soon as possible to sift out and recognize the relevance of the points they present.

Freedom of expression must be exercised finally in a climate charged with a certain purposefulness. A definite subject or problem must be selected as a focus around which this atmosphere of freedom of expression can revolve. The leader tries to hold the group participants on the subject but tries not to direct their thinking. Also, the participants should develop common stated goals in the early stages of the Plan. Some of these goals should be related to the subjects of discussion so that all participants will share common reasons for exploring these subjects. These goals can be another means of self-discipline by which participants can make creative use of freedom of expression.

Expression gradually changes from a more or less undisciplined "gabfest" at the beginning of the learning experience to a frank, free, and purposeful discussion among persons who accept each other as adults striving, each in his peculiar way, to bring into some meaningful relationship the aspects of the subject being discussed. If the leaders and group participants have stimulated intelligent questioning, separated the wheat from the chaff in the questions and discussions, and encouraged persons to work freely with each other, an observer will likely notice, as the program develops, that the participants have added to their store of factual knowledge as well as learned more about living with one another as Christians.

4. Effective Communication is Essential

Communication is our link with others; it prevents us from being either partially or wholly isolated, and of course inhibits the inevitable results of isolation -- a sort of a shrinking or drying up of our personalities. Recognizing the fact that we are social beings, we must cultivate the skills necessary to improve our relationships with others through effective communication with them. To many persons communication has come to mean largely a one-way process involving one person's telling or transmitting information to others. In a modern sense it seldom seems to connote sharing, although one of the original meanings of the word was "to share." A dictionary labels this meaning archaic now.

Communication as used here, however, should be understood to mean a sharing of ideas, thoughts, and feelings between and

31

among people. It is a two-way process; not telling or imparting alone but also receiving. Without reception the situation is analogous to a radio station whose potential audience either does not have a receiving set or keeps the one it owns turned off. Certainly there is no communication here, because no one is reached. We, as learners, are not always "tuned in" even though we happen to be physically present where and when we are supposed to learn.

If there is no communication, there is no learning. The one who speaks cannot do the whole job; the receiver must have his **"set"** turned on. Actually, however, the most effective learning will take place when both speaker and hearer assume a new role, that of being both receivers and transmitters. It is easier to keep the "set" turned on when the one who ordinarily plays the part of receiver sees himself in the new role and accepts the dual responsibility for listening and also for sharing what he knows with others. The art of communication is learned by the individual with the help of his fellow learners. And as communication improves in any kind of learning situation, so usually does the quality of what is learned.

5. <u>Values Which Can Accrue from Freedom of Expression</u>
a. <u>We understand more about how to learn together.</u> When we are encouraged to express ourselves and are intelligently helped toward disciplined expression by those with whom we are learning, we can begin to understand ourselves better and also those persons with whom we are learning. Persistent effort is required of all those in the learning group to accept each other as human beings and to bring themselves into a constantly improving relationship with God and each other. Acceptance of each other does not imply the condoning of each other's shortcomings (it is highly doubtful whether most of us can objectively identify the shortcomings of others). Acceptance is rather a recognition that shortcomings are part of each unique personality and that each person must struggle with the problems peculiar to him as he is able.

As we become better acquainted and begin to feel the impact of purposeful association, three enemies of productive learning -- fear, suspicion, and pride -- become increasingly inoperative. Corporate learning then becomes increasingly effective.

b. Our ability to communicate is improved. As the learner begins to recognize the group as a learning team which he must help and from which he can get help and acceptance, he feels easier about expressing his ideas. As frustration and defensiveness diminish, creative learning results. This forward movement results partly through better communication -- a more complete cycle of understanding between the one who expresses himself and those who are better able to put meaning into what he says.

c. We establish a climate for learning. Learning takes place when certain conditions exist. One of these significant conditions which affect learning is the way the learners feel. For example, (1) some may dislike the leader; (2) some may be exhausted or feel under par physically; (3) some may have had trouble just before they came to the adult education meeting; (4) some may and others may not want the clergyman present; (5) one person may dislike another in the group and even without verbal expression or sharp glances, other participants will absorb the tension to such an extent that it strongly affects the learning situation; (6) a remark made by one may be taken as a personal affront by another who feels a strong need to be respected. All these situations and countless others may work together to create barriers to productive learning; learning which helps us to know God better in order to better serve Him. Surely we are able to tackle our learning problems more directly and enthusiastically in an atmosphere of respect and love than in a climate saturated with fear, pride, and suspicion. In the learning group is a good place to start making cooperation, human dignity and love more than high-sounding words.

The few conditions listed above which help create a negative learning climate may not seem logical or reasonable. Unfortunately logic or reason does not always play a decisive role, particularly in the opening act of this learning drama. Feeling seems to be the leading factor at first and is important throughout the process. Feelings must be released. Through freedom of expression tensions are relieved, and this clearing of the stage for action is also important -- as important as any action which will follow.

d. **We learn to know ourselves and each other better.** One of the problems sometimes wholly ignored in the teaching-learning process is our need to know as much as we can about ourselves and about those with whom we are learning. Too often we wish immediately to "get at the heart of the problem" or to "come to grips" with the subject without considering that people are involved, that the subject under consideration is in itself static until it takes on life and meaning through people. By our impatience to get on with the learning, we unknowingly inhibit it.

Before we learners can meaningfully attack this problem, we must learn, for example, why we are stubborn to a point where we refuse to listen carefully to others, and why we quickly reject new ideas and new ways to approach old ideas. This problem of learning about self and others, which requires some self-examination, is as important as learning about subject matter, because it often affects how we interpret subject matter. The two should be approached together. Sometimes we resist coming to know people and becoming acquainted with their ideas because new ideas may disturb our present organization of self. We must try to understand, as a leader, or a group participant, that often we come to an educational meeting with our fellow churchmen not to learn but to try to get support for our ego through a pet idea we have long held as hallowed.

It is essential, therefore, for all members of the learning team to make persistent and sincere efforts to learn how to accept people as human beings who have problems, some of which may make learning difficult for them. We must recognize that

each facet of our behavior has some meaning and learn to interpret it in ourselves and others. For instance, there is a reason why a person bites his fingernails, and usually it is not
for the purpose of shortening his nails. All behavior represents some motivation, and understanding of it may help us to
mature.

Of course, information can be transmitted from a speaker
to a listener without either the speaker or the listener having
to become acquainted with each other. However, a task of adult
religious education is not only to transmit information but also
to develop, in the process, a Christian relationship among
those who participate. This relationship brings into meaning
the church as a corporate body -- a body of people learning to
live, to work, and to worship corporately. Actually the purpose
of adult religious education is realized when, to as great an
extent as possible, the subject matter is put to use as it is
learned. And one of the most essential uses to which adult
religious education can be applied is as an aid in identifying
our roles as individuals and in learning how each of us can use
his valuable and unique talents to work together toward common
goals. The feeling of oneness with humanity, and thoughtful
action based on that feeling, is essential if adult religious
education programs are to amount to anything more than academic
exercises in the Scripture or social discussion programs.

e. We discover that freedom is essential to creative learning.
Learning is of many kinds. Oliver Twist learned to pick people's pockets efficiently. Given freedom, we can learn how to
hurt people by using all sorts of weapons -- such as bombs,
sharp words, guns. These are examples of learning of sorts.
This freedom can result in decisions which are a curse or a
blessing, much as water can sustain human life or destroy it.
We have the choice to make.

Effective use of freedom can result in creative learning.
But we must learn to distinguish between free and honest expression and blunt, sarcastic and crude remarks. Such remarks
often signify insecurity rather than freedom. Freedom in a

learning group involves the risk of making mistakes, but it also involves the satisfaction of success. The newness and freshness of creative thought can blossom fully when we emphasize accepting people for what they are rather than praising or blaming them. Fear of criticism or saying the "wrong" things helps prevent creativity.

f. We have something to say about the forces which shape our minds. History records the continuing struggle of people who are determined to have something to say about what happens to them in society. As history reveals the evolution of the idea of democracy ("democracy" means people's rule) through more than two thousand years, it points to the seemingly perpetual conflict between two groups: those who feel they know what is good for people and "the people" themselves, who wish to have a strong voice in determining their own destiny. As always, there are those who feel that the people cannot be trusted, or at least cannot be trusted at some particular time or with some particular issue. These are the dictators and the autocrats of our own and other countries of the world, against whom the people are waging a continuous struggle.

Authoritarianism still, to a large degree, controls people's education. In too many cases where voluntary programs of a rigid nature are set up in churches, colleges, and evening schools, the "students" do not appear in large numbers. Then, more often than not, follow the usual analyses of the situation which end with the conclusion that (1) people are not interested in learning anything and (2) you can depend on only a few people anyway.

In many cases the potential learners are not to blame. The failure is often due to the fact that, from beginning to end of the planning, rarely, if ever, were the people involved. They probably had nothing to say about the subject matter, the procedures, or the place and time of the meetings. They were not interested in the program because it was not their program. They must feel close to the program; they must feel it is theirs, that they are having something to say about the educational forces which to some extent shape their destinies.

g. **We** can **recognize** a **new** relationship **to** the **congregational family**. During the early stages of a series of educational meetings one participant stated that he couldn't see that forgiveness, as he was taught it, had anything to do with him. A tomb-like quietness fell upon the group. The participants had not reached the stage in their development which permitted them to feel that they would be accepted by each other. Therefore they refrained from commenting on this outburst. The very nature of the situation, the awful silence which fell on this group of eighteen people, clearly indicated that something was wrong. Should this person have made such a comment about a vital religious point? Did other persons in the group feel the same way but fear to express their feelings?

Before the next meeting date five persons from the group made a special effort to see the person who made the original comment, not as a group but individually. They told him that they had had similar feelings on the matter. Now, at least six in the group of eighteen had indicated that forgiveness was only a theological term to them. The six people thought there were probably others in the group who did not wish to expose their ignorance on the matter and, therefore, had chosen to remain silent. Their suppositions proved true. At the following meeting, encouraged by support he received from the five persons who talked with him, the man who first spoke of forgiveness brought it up again.

Before the meeting ended, twelve members of the group, by some sort of comment, revealed that forgiveness did not seem to have the real impact in their religious life that they thought it should have.

This discovery did two important things:

(1) It clearly indicated to nearly all of the participants that they had problems in common through which they could share

experiences and learn how to work together toward meaningful solutions.

(2) It helped the participants to begin to function freely as a learning team rather than as a number of isolated individuals.

6. Dangers of Improper Use of Freedom of Expression

Most things can be misused. Freedom of expression is no exception. Freedom of expression is a vital condition of adult learning, but that freedom, if it is not disciplined freedom, may result in dominance by one or several participants to the point where others are discouraged from taking part. The trainer, the volunteer leader, and the group participants themselves, must guard against these dangers which may result from unlimited freedom of speech. Since all participants are trained to work together as a team, and to evaluate their process regularly, the danger of misusing freedom is lessened.

a. Misunderstanding of discipline. Improper use of freedom through misunderstanding of discipline can cause freedom of expression to be ineffective. A limited discipline brings order into a learning situation. But where should the discipline come from? A well-conducted learning program which encourages self-discipline is a positive step toward growth in responsibility. That type of learning program which imposes excessive discipline by a leader encourages excessive dependency.

Development toward maturity in thinking and acting is encouraged by helping each other to realize our responsibility for the statements we make as well as for the deeds we perform. Freedom to say what we think must be balanced by our willingness to be responsible for what we say. Just as we have many other privileges which are balanced by responsibilities, so with freedom of expression. This involves our willingness to make the effort necessary to learn increasing self-discipline and thus to lessen the need for discipline from without.

b. Talking without Purpose. If members of a beginning group are allowed time enough, without any direction, they usually

38

talk themselves out on a friendly but superficial basis. But after this they become restless and irritated and then trouble begins. Free expression at this point may result in conflict which will break up the group. When we have nothing we recognize as purposeful to do and yet think we ought to be doing something worthwhile, we are developing a conflict within ourselves. When fifteen or twenty persons are going through a similar experience, striving to find some outlet for a growing internal conflict, it soon becomes a big external one. Since it is not socially acceptable to engage in physical combat, we see the more expedient outlet and "lay each other out" with our tongues.

c. Standardizing of ideas. Some of us are more articulate than others, have had more experience expressing our thoughts and feelings, or at least are not as reluctant to talk about them as some of our fellow learners. These persons to some degree have an advantage over those of us who find verbal expression difficult.

Articulate persons are sometimes overpersuasive, causing cooperation or unity which is false because it is premature or inadequately grounded. In such cases of apparent agreement individuality is often thwarted because many fruitful ideas and/or learning problems never are expressed. Then, too, some of us would rather "cooperate" with somebody else's plan or idea than exercise our own thinking and offer our own ideas. We must guard against pursuing unity and cooperation with such vigor and enthusiasm that some of the persons on the learning team feel that it is easier or safer to cooperate than to think. More and more of us must be encouraged and stimulated to offer suggestions, to help plan, to question intelligently and without malice the views and plans others offer which we don't understand.

Even ideas which we feel are not particularly good ones must be kindly acknowledged if we are to help each other to learn to offer better ones. We have to start some place, and many persons have had few places to start where embarrassment or even fear did not dominate the scene. Fear of parents, fear of the boss, or fear of someone who might jeopardize social standing play such strong roles that learning to be free is next to impossible in many cases. No more important place exists than the church for attacking in a straightforward manner this powerful and effective inhibitor to learning.

Impatience with persons who have been accustomed to leaning on other people results when we are overly zealous about developing unity and cooperation. Those of us who have not learned to do our share of independent thinking are often too willing to fall back into our old behavior pattern and let others do the thinking. When we are encouraged to think through problems we must be allowed the time necessary for this sometimes unusual and rather difficult experience. Those of us who think more slowly, or have never been helped to think through a problem, may need much time. The pressure of the zealot confuses us. When we learn how to attack a problem, and learn further that our opinions are respected by others, we begin to feel more comfortable in the group and a more effective learning situation results.

SECTION C

ACTIVE INDIVIDUAL PARTICIPATION

1. Introduction

Active individual participation is expressed by participants who actively assume the responsibilities for the various tasks which must be performed to insure the success of the cooperative learning endeavor. Although learning can take place without verbal participation, we are concerned in the Plan with a way of learning in which active physical and verbal participation, as well as listening, play important roles.

Participation is an essential activity through which we can learn to take our share of responsibility. But often we don't know how or when to use it; therefore, we need some instructions. The training that is offered during the Starting Phase of this Plan[2] helps to prepare us for making the best use of active participation. In these training sessions, we learn a few of the mechanics of group participation and leadership. Then we learn how to participate effectively by participating, by accepting specific responsibilities and evaluating the effects of participating.

2. Results of Being Told

We have been lectured and talked down to by others most of our lives -- in homes, schools, and churches. Sometimes this kind of instruction is necessary. Most of the time it is overdone. There are two important results of this approach with which we must deal in this program: dependency and rebellion.

a. Many of us have become dependent on the "teller." We feel a lack of confidence in ourselves because the "teller" knows so much and we so little. This dependence sometimes grows until we are fearful that almost anything we say could be said so much better by someone else that we say little or nothing. We have become fearful, and fear is no ally of creative learning. We have always had someone tell us, and it is quite natural to do nothing and wait for the same thing to happen here and now.

Even after some training in how to participate, we sometimes continue to sit in meetings and wait for a teacher or someone else to tell us. Occasionally some members of the learning team will take advantage of this reluctance of those who want to be told, and will start to "tell" them. This, of course, is what the fearful member wants. He is relieved of a share of responsibility. Now he can sit back and fall into

_____

[2]See Chapter III.

his old behavior pattern. The teller also may welcome this opportunity because he can again express his desire to run things autocratically. Neither of these persons up to this point has learned what responsible participation is.

The "teller" sometimes doesn't wish to wait until the "listener" has a chance to establish himself in a climate that is conducive to learning -- where fear plays a minor role. He wants to get work done! The "teller" is not willing to find out at first what the listener doesn't know or is possibly too shy to express. But unless we find out what we don't know as well as what we do, effective group participation and individual learning can't take place.

How do we discover what we don't know? The first step is to establish an atmosphere in which we feel that our free expression will receive respectful consideration. The would-be-learner is often as responsible as the self appointed "teller" for the break-down of this idea of learning together. This point can be illustrated in the case of the patient who goes to the physician. The physician asks him what's wrong and the patient replies, "You're the doctor. That's what I came to find out."

b. Another result of this overemphasis on being told by someone else is rebellion. The person who has been "told" and restricted may react quite differently -- and often does -- when he is given new freedom. He may sit back and sort of dare a leader or teacher to do anything with him. He may use the same techniques which were used on him so that he can try to escape the control he felt. When he uses these autocratic techniques in a group learning situation, we have somewhat of a problem. This person is in a sense protecting himself from control by exercising it on others.

Both the overpassive person and the overzealous group member are obvious drawbacks to programs based on active individual participation. That is one reason why training in participation teamwork is necessary. But productive participation develops gradually, and as a result of our active efforts, not rapidly or automatically.

Adult **learning** situations **which** involve active individual participation **are** often **more** difficult to manage than a teacher-student arrangement. They also can be more productive. More can happen to the participants. We **can** learn subject matter and how to make it meaningful and useful. We can learn about ourselves and about our fellow learners because we have to work closely with them, not just sit next to them. We have many opportunities to learn how to accept responsibility by accepting it. We have a very large share of the job to do ourselves. This job cannot be done for us by a leader or teacher.

3. Articulation of Feelings

In this Plan it is important to express our feelings about the subject and the learning process as honestly and frankly as we can. The process of pouring ourselves out by saying how we feel about a matter can help us to conquer fear, help others to know how to help us, and sometimes help us to identify and clear away stumbling blocks to our own learning. Because we are in part emotional beings, the kind of learning which helps us to mature is difficult unless and until we look at ourselves and see what stops us from learning.

Often at the beginning of this process, when we are trying to adjust to each other and develop a cooperative learning attitude, we are disturbed. We feel that nothing real is taking place. It appears that these honest expressions of feelings and sometimes false conceptions are

43

fruitless. But under a competent trainer's direction we can advance as a learning team. We start much like a building already built. First, the contractor examines the structure and finds what is wrong. He then substitutes for worn-out and decaying timbers newer and stronger ones. He clears out as much faulty material as he can, without jeopardizing the building itself. This whole job is simpler for the building contractor than it is for the learner, because building materials are inanimate.

We frequently resist change or new ideas to a point where it nearly destroys us. Under favorable conditions, however, we can and do grow. Honest and humble expression of our feelings and beliefs, without fear of being thought naive and stupid by our fellow learners, is one way to start. To get the soil loosened so that we begin to express ourselves productively requires the competent guidance of a trainer (the person who sets this Plan in motion and guides the training activities). The trainer promotes the development of free expression and effective discussion teamwork. Also he encourages us to discover corporately and personally our weak spots which inhibit productive learning.

4. Using Educational Terminology
In the Indiana Plan we learn to become a learning team. We find out something about how we learn by actually engaging in a learning process. We learn more about a specific area of subject matter at the same time that we improve our relationships with others and our ability to learn.

It is not, however, the purpose of this Plan to make all participants amateur psychologists. Such words as identification, incorporation, projection, which will be used here, are merely to help the reader to recognize certain ways we all behave so he can recognize success and failure in informal learning and also trace the evolution of a

44

successful learning pattern. Sometimes these new words, or
old words which seem to have a new meaning, are overly fas-
cinating for us. The insights they afford are tools to help
us to put what talent we have to the task of helping ourselves
and others to learn productively as Christians.

Tossing new words around in the learning groups does
little good and often irritates participants. We should
express what we mean in language people understand. One
certain way to inhibit a learning group is to make the participants overly conscious of technical terms. ("Did you
identify with this person?") Of course, there are many
other ways to ruin the program, but here is one ready-made.
The trainer can wreck it merely by turning the learning program into a pseudo-psychological clinic. Sound learning
principles and a few needed descriptive terms are useful,
but trainers and leaders do not practice group therapy any
more than they would try to practice medicine.

5. <u>Some Useful Educational Terms</u>
As we actively participate several factors usually emerge
that are described by certain concepts. These concepts
aren't just academic terms. They are real factors in group
behavior. If the terms are understood and constructively
used, they help people to understand the significance of
their active participation. The result is a better understanding of self and others and growth toward Christian
maturity. At the end of this section is a chart called "A
Pattern of Learning That Leads to Change." This chart can
assist the reader to see the relationships of the following
terms in the educational process.

a. <u>Ambivalence</u>. The existence of contradictory feelings
at the same time with respect to the same object or situation is called ambivalence. It is evident in all of
us at one time or another when we are faced with ideas
which threaten our present attitudes and behaviors. We
believe, yet we don't believe; we think we love, and yet

45

at the same time we have a feeling of hate; we want to
take an active part in the group learning situation, yet
we want to withdraw from it into a more secure and comfortable situation.

This sort of yes-and-no, wanting-and-not-wanting
situation causes us emotional conflict. We try to resolve these conflicts by making decisions. The way we
make these decisions is important.

If we are sufficiently objective, we can learn from
one another to examine carefully, evaluate, and weigh
the opposing feelings which give substance to ambivalence.
We then are better equipped to make an intelligent decision based primarily on emotion.

The trainer, leaders, and group participants in
this learning program are responsible for helping each
other, but they cannot make decisions for one another
to resolve ambivalence. This is a job each person must
do himself. Each participant must learn to grow by re-
solving these emotional conflicts and standing back of
his decisions.

b.   Projection, Rationalization, Identification, and Incorporation. Tension exists in us to a degree in any situation which seems to require us to make adjustment and
change. Sometimes we try to adjust to our problems by
blaming others; by placing the burden of responsibility
on other persons or on the circumstances of a situation.
We relieve ourselves of responsibility. This way of
reacting is called projection.

We tend to settle down into a habitual way of thinking, feeling and acting, and we don't want to change.
The person or group who tries to change us we often regard as a threat, because we tend to resent any attempt
to get us to reorganize our present attitudes. We tend
to protect ourselves as we now are. We have many ways

of saying, in effect, "I am going to stay the way I am; I will not change." For example, we sometimes use persuasion, argument, and even physical force. We don't want to change because change means disturbance within us. If there is to be struggle, we prefer to direct it outward against somebody else rather than to deal with it internally ourselves. But we must deal with it internally if we are to experience growth in relationship with others. Learning -- making constructive changes in our attitudes and behavior -- is a personal problem.

A common method of self-defense is the struggle we sometimes put up to find a "reason" for not doing something we ought to do. This is called rationalization. We try to project anger, irritation, anxiety, and fear into excuses and arguments in such a way as would appear reasonable to others and ourselves. It is a way of refusing to look honestly at ourselves or to examine ideas which will threaten our present behaviors, opinions, and feelings.

One way of adjusting to conflict is to identify with other persons. When we accept (see Acceptance) a person as a fellow human being, we prepare the way for identifying with him. In this sense acceptance is static -- we are getting ourselves ready to do something. Then as we attempt further to understand sincerely the person, we enter into a dynamic relationship -- we become identified with him in order to bring about a better understanding. Unless this process takes place, we will find it difficult honestly and sincerely to give a fair hearing to others. If we are merely being polite and not really listening and trying to understand, we are avoiding a potential learning situation for us and for our fellow learners. We are falling into a vicious trap by assuming the attitude, "If I can't see where I can get anything out of this, I'm not interested." Corporate learning fails here.

There are actually two sides to the coin which we call identification. One is that we identify with others because we like them. They act and think the way we do. When this takes place we don't have to do much reorganizing of ourselves to meet them halfway. People whom we like do not represent a serious threat to the present organization of ourselves. The other side of the coin is that we can develop a link with another who has a different point of view. But when we try to become identified with those who hold views different from ours, we must yield somewhat; we must reorganize our feelings. Here is where conflict sometimes enters, tempting us to defend rather than examine our present organization of self-interest in our decisions and actions.

Rationalization, projection, identification, and incorporation work together as part of a learning process. After we discover the ways in which we defend ourselves, and why we do it, then we can move forward from immature methods of adjustment into a bond of common feeling which can be a result of identification. The learners can help each other to resolve the personal internal struggles (ambivalence) between their established ideas and a new way of thinking and feeling through this identification. When the learners begin to understand the new ideas and stop struggling against each other, they are beginning to learn. When they understand the new idea, it becomes part of them. This is called incorporation. We move from conflict and self-defense toward identification and incorporation.

We need each other. As we learn together by intelligently yielding some of ourselves to others, we grow in union and understanding. We begin to think of our

fellow humans as persons who need our help and understanding, even if we disagree with some of their views.

When we make an honest effort to identify with
others, we will, of course, run into some disappointments.
Then we may want to project again by blaming someone or
some circumstances. The urge for satisfaction in this
way can now be stopped because we recognize what projection is and what shifting blame and responsibility means
to us and to others. We are learning how to break a
habit, to change our behavior -- in short, we are growing.

c. Resistance. We live in a world of change, yet we tend
to resist it. Part of the learning task is to help us
accept change; to help us realize that we are part of a
moving, active world. We can learn this in dynamic situations in which we become involved.

Some teachers give lip service to the factor of
participation in learning, by permitting the group to
engage in a question and answer period after a lecture.
Very little of either participation or resistance will
be noted in this process. Most students will settle into
a comfortable spot and believe, temporarily at least,
that they have discovered a haven of peace. But this
security pattern is not productive. The learners are
not allowed to defend themselves by expressing their
resistance, which expression is often an early step in
the movement of learning (see chart, "A Pattern of
Learning that Leads to Change," at the end of this
section.)

Now in a well-organized plan which involves free
participation, the learners would have an opportunity to
express their resistance actively and to be accepted
as they are. Probably several members of the learning
team are aware of this need. So the learners who feel
threatened by an idea are encouraged to disagree, to

assert themselves, to express their resistances. Now it will be noted that the learners often experience these conflicts on a person-to-person basis. But they cannot satisfactorily resolve their conflict by fighting against each other, because this is a form of escape that allows them to avoid facing the learning problem within. They continue to assert themselves as they are.

Some latitude should be allowed for the learners to defend themselves; if it is allowed to continue too long, however, the goal may become that of trying to prove someone right and someone wrong. At this point the perceptive leader or group participants help their fellow-learners in conflict to struggle with the idea and not against persons. This means that the learners are now helping each other to understand and come to terms with the idea within themselves.

Resistance may express itself in different ways. The following two reactions are the most common forms of active resistance in group learning situations, which group participants and leaders must be prepared to recognize and meet:

We may withdraw;
We may resist by aggressive acts.

The person who is trying to find a way to express his disagreement may refrain from all active participation. He may just sit, and when the leader or another participant tries to get his attention by looking in his direction, he will look at the table, or at somebody else. He feels he must resist any attempt to make an inroad into his well-established ideas. So he sits in silence -- he tries to withdraw from the group.

It should be made clear that this situation is everybody's problem and that they are to help each other to come to some understanding. A question might be directed to the one who is trying to withdraw. He is encouraged and helped to participate, but not forced to do so. Participation is the key to return him to the group as an active learner. So a calm and reasonable effort is made to help him to participate again. Of course, swarming upon the one who withdraws will not produce the results desired. He may interpret too much effort as indicating his relative importance in the group. If we "baby" him, we aren't helping him to grow toward maturity. He must learn to recognize that he must accept the group, not just expect the group to accept him. Time is sometimes an ally here.

We cannot succeed with the person who tries to withdraw by simply demanding his active participation -- by insisting that he "return to the group." We can often help and encourage him by asking what he thinks about the problem under consideration; by being pleasant and cheerful; by allowing him to blow off steam when he finally decides to return.

The one who withdraws, therefore, must be helped by the leader and other participants to recognize:

(1) That his help is needed in the group.

(2) That he is not going to be treated as a special character at the expense of his fellow-learners.

(3) That the other participants want to help him.

(4) That it is sometimes painful to grow and mature.

(5) That every individual has a personal responsibility for the success of the corporate venture.

(6) That we finally have to come to grips with our problems within ourselves. We can't get rid of the conflict satisfactorily by lashing out at others or by saying and doing nothing.

(7) That sympathy alone will not do the job. Understanding help is offered, but the participant is given the opportunity to determine whether or not he wants this help.

We might try to resist (protect ourselves from change) by being aggressive. We might burst out with a tirade to try to frighten those persons who seem to be a threat to us and to the organization of ourselves (our attitudes and beliefs). Patient understanding is useful here. If participants try to answer this aggressive move with more aggression it usually results in fruitless arguments and ill will.

d. <u>Acceptance</u>. Acceptance is something we learn when we begin to think of each other as fellow human beings who behave in a certain manner for specific reasons. Their behavior may be acceptable to society or it may be quite unacceptable.

Acceptance does not mean necessarily that we approve of a person's conduct. When we go to a physician with a broken arm, he doesn't approve or disapprove of the condition of the arm. It is broken; that's a fact. So he tries to help nature to mend it.

We need not approve of a person's conduct or manners in order to accept him as a person in his own right -- a fellow who probably could use a lot of help from an understanding co-learner.

We need to understand what acceptance means because it has something important to do with the growth of our Christian relationships with other persons. We must learn to accept others as individuals, as unique personalities. This is important if we are to make our unique contribution toward the progress and growth of the learning team.

e. <u>Rejection</u>. Productive learning takes place best when we're ready to learn, when we are interested in what we are doing, when we want to do it, and when we feel right about the people with whom we are learning. This latter condition means that we want to feel that we belong in

the group, that we are accepted as a fellow learner. It
is the job of the trainer, and later of the leaders and
group participants, to help learners to feel that they
are wanted.

Rejection is a feeling. It can come about in several ways. In a group learning situation a person may
begin to feel rejected when:

(1) He is ignored.

(2) He feels that his comments and efforts are not
    appreciated.

(3) He sees people carrying on side conversations
    and whispering while he is talking. This might
    be indicative to the speaker that his remarks
    aren't of much value.

(4) He is constantly interrupted by others -- not
    by questions, but by persons who are trying to
    dispute or add to his comments.

(5) People do not appear to listen to him.

(6) He is sharply cut off when he tries to make a
    comment.

(7) His comments are listened to in a condescending
    manner, then ignored.

Any one or combination of these reactions is sometimes enough to lose a potential learner, particularly
one who is sensitive. We can't stand to feel not wanted
-- rejected. Different persons react differently. Some
will ignore a large part, or all, of a situation which
makes others feel rejected. Sometimes we may feel rejected when the cause of the feeling was not consciously
attributable to any person. Other times some members of
the group deliberately cause others to feel rejected.
This happens more particularly when the group is new.
It is an evidence of insecurity and poor teamwork which
must be overcome.

So we really have the problem of sometimes actually being rejected and sometimes only feeling that we are on the outside when no effort was made to put us there. In both cases, however, it is our feelings which must be dealt with. One effective way to mutual understanding is to get these feelings out in the open. Until we can talk over our relationships in God's family, we aren't going to make much progress toward the goal of effective adult religious education.

In early meetings feelings of rejection may occur quite often. In the beginning stages we are becoming adjusted; we are restless, a little uncomfortable and on edge at times. As we begin to mature in this program we learn to work together and to respect one another as fellow beings and to share each other's learning problems.

f. Recognition. Recognition as used here is closely allied to the process of discovery. The more we are involved in the discovery of our educational needs, the better we can discern and meet them. We are more likely to act when we have a stake in the proceedings. It is important, therefore, for us to explore together and help each other identify these needs. We must discover a need and have a strong desire to satisfy that need if something worthwhile is to happen to us.

Symptomatic needs will almost inevitably be expressed during the first few meetings. We will talk about subjects we think we need to discuss or that we want others to believe we need to discuss. These suppositions may be only a part of what we actually need. Unless together in the early stages of the program, we continue to analyze needs carefully, we are likely to base the Starting Phase of the Plan on so-called "felt needs," which often have little or no basis in fact. The "felt needs," however, often provide a starting point toward the recognition of real needs.

We must begin with an awareness that we are trying to satisfy our real learning needs, but that quite often these real needs are not immediately recognizable. They are sometimes disguised by our own lack of understanding, our lack of insight.

In the Starting Phase of the Indiana Plan (and again in the Expanding Phase) we try to recognize some of the religious educational needs we hold in common while working together as a learning team. As needs are considered and the related problems exposed, they may not be precisely what an expert would diagnose. But "experts" must learn to accept this as a part of the process of putting as much responsibility as possible on the learner for inquiry and discovery. As far as possible the learners work their own way through this need-discovering process, slowly and creatively.

Others can tell us what they think we need. Sometimes they are right. But unless we believe they are right, we follow blindly or not at all. We begin to prepare ourselves for recognition by becoming intimately involved in a learning process in which we play a major role in discovering and facing our real educational needs. We can discern some of these needs by constantly evaluating and refining the process of discovery. We must use every resource possible (expert opinion, reading materials, our own experience, discussion with others who may be in the same situation), but finally we have to make up our minds in terms of something we can understand. In the last analysis, the learner must recognize the need as having meaning for him, before very much genuine change can take place in his behavior.

However much we might hope to attain our Christian growth rapidly, our maturation doesn't develop that way. We change slowly, which is another way of saying that we shouldn't expect to recognize our real needs quickly.

We can learn and remember certain dates and some factual information with comparative ease. But the learning which causes us to adjust our way of life, to review our outlook, to examine our job as co-workers in the family of God, takes time and patience -- and sometimes causes discomfort.

We try to recognize, then, among other things: (1) our real educational needs; (2) the nature of ourselves -- the meaning of what we feel; and (3) we try to see ourselves as we really are in relation to others. These are vital points in this process of learning. We are not to examine ideas or facts alone, but ideas and facts in actual relationship to our unique selves and to our fellow learners.

A PATTERN OF LEARNING THAT LEADS TO CHANGE

1. This is What Learners Often Have CONFLICT	2. This is What Learners Often Do to Resolve Conflict DEFENSE	3. This is What Learners Should Do To Learn Together Creatively RESOLVE THE CONFLICT	4. This is the Result of Creative Learning INCORPORATION
Learner feels need for change, yet wishes to remain as he is when faced with ideas that threaten his present attitudes and behavior. This ambivalence is a conflict between "the old," and "the new." It creates tension in the learner. He must resolve the conflict.	Learner defends himself against ideas that force him to admit his limitations; resists the will of someone else or something to change him. Defense may take some of the following forms:	Learner struggles with himself — the new way of thinking and feeling vs. his habitual ways. People can help each other in this struggle to try to understand a new idea objectively if they work together as a team. The original ambivalence is examined objectively and cooperatively.	Learner understands, accepts and assimilates the new point of view
NOTE: When the need for change is readily apparent, learners sometimes resolve this conflict by passing rapidly to Steps 3 and 4.	Projection—we defend our present ideas by asserting ourselves as we now are, by blaming somebody or some circumstances. Rationalization — we become angry, we withdraw, or we don't listen actively in order to protect ourselves.	The learner himself must make the decision to learn: the learner is free to face the ambivalence within himself (1) when no one insists on changing him; (2) when he can express himself freely; (3) when he feels accepted regardless of his attitude; (4) when he is not attacked or put on the defensive as a person.	
	NOTE: Productive change rarely comes about by a conflict of wills in the attempt to prove somebody right and somebody wrong.	The process of incorporation is aided by the identification of individual learners with the other members of the learning team.	

SECTION D

SHARING IN PROGRAM DEVELOPMENT

1. Introduction

One of the first steps in the Indiana Plan involves the participants in developing the educational program. Ultimately participants share in identifying their needs, setting goals, choosing
resources, choosing appropriate educational methods, and out-
lining the program. To many persons this is a new departure--
a departure so completely new and different that many will meet
it with suspicion and resistance unless evolutionary procedures
are followed.

2. Education in Transition

The idea behind learners becoming intimately involved in every
phase of the educational program should be briefly considered.
For centuries we have been exposed to a system of education
which has in some cases tended to ignore the creative nature of
the learner. Too often the teacher prescribes the learning
needs for adult learners, without giving them the opportunity
to recognize those needs. Some teachers work with a group of
potential learners as if they were all quite the same--the
same in abilities, the same in interests, the same in physical
and emotional health.

Modern adults have been brought up under an educational
system in transition. In the days before mass education, the
learner was usually in very close contact with the teacher.
Over the years a learner often developed intellectually, spir-
itually, and socially as a result of long, intimate association
with good teachers and with small groups of learners.

Today's adult has been exposed to a kind of mass education
in the making. But, as in many worthwhile things, there are
inherent dangers in mass education. In many instances the
student is lectured to most of the time. He is told when to be
present, what he should know, and how long he must go to school.

His courses are often too carefully planned _for_ him (with here and there some "elective" as a concession to liberal thought on educational matters).

Too often our educational system attempts to tell us that freedom is our heritage, that in order to remain strong and free, we must accept responsibility. In his religious education, also, the adult has been told and catechized. And as a result he is assumed to be ready to take his part as an active, dynamic, God-respecting citizen of a free state. We have been _told_ how to do all these things, but few opportunities have been offered for us to learn by practicing the art of living while we are learning.

What effect has all this telling had on us? The more we are told, the more we expect to be told. Telling is effective to a degree. When carried to an extreme, as too often happens, telling becomes the antithesis of adult learning. People can't teach us by constantly telling us to be responsible, to follow the good and the true, to be free. Few lasting results come from their effort. But when we become actively involved in developing and maintaining our jobs, homes, religion, and government, we come face to face with actual situations and have an opportunity to learn how to stand on our own feet. Responsibility is learned through actual and dynamic situations. We learn more about our religion by being actively involved in it: by studying it, by discussing it, by feeling it, by practicing it. We must develop educational situations that make these agents possible.

It is sometimes argued that an adult religious education program, such as the Indiana Plan, in which people are of prime concern, (a) takes too much time waiting until the people understand it and accept responsibility, and (b) can't be effective because people who don't know can't arrive at any answers--they need to be told.

Those who object on the time basis have as much of it as anybody else. It will be observed that usually these persons have not taken the time to study and understand the program. Regardless of the time it takes, the learner's understanding is basic. If we can't wait till he understands, it's pretty obvious he's not going to learn effectively.

On the second point, those of us who believe that telling alone is the prime method of teaching are vain. We are flattering ourselves. We don't really teach much by telling. Reading, studying, observing, sharing ideas by discussion, listening (which is the other end of telling)--all are important factors in helping us to learn. Telling is but one factor. It is perhaps the easiest way to try to transmit, or at least to expose, certain kinds of information to large numbers of persons in a short period of time.

A difficult problem presents itself at this point. We who have had little to do with determining what we should do and how we shall do it are content to remain, like the canary, in captivity. We want to come right back to the cage when taken out of it. We will not always help as much as we can to develop a program in which we must face up to responsibilities. We don't want to get out of our favorite chair or make any change. A school official once said, when asked to make available a program for adults, "I've been here twenty years. In five more years I'll retire, and I don't want any trouble with new things between now and then."

When a good leader is asked for the answer to a problem, he usually asks, "What do you think?" In other words, he puts the responsibility right back where it belongs: on the members of the learning team. Of course, this example is more suited to group discussion. And complete programs of adult education involve many more group procedures than group discussion. The basic idea, however, is the same in all situations. No matter what procedure is used--the responsibility for determining the nature of the program and how it is to be handled should be in

60

the hands of trained adult learners. This responsibility gives
learners a twofold opportunity: (1) to learn about the subject
area which the group has decided to pursue, and (2) to learn
better ways to explore the subject area.

3. Why Learners Should Share
    in Program Development
    a. We need to feel that the educational program and ob-
jective are ours. Most of us take more interest in and better
care of something that we feel is ours; for instance, an owner
of a house usually takes better care of it than a tenant.

We must be helped to feel that the educational program is
ours. Telling us that it is our program is one thing. Assist-
ing us to discover our real learning needs, and to satisfy
those needs through the intelligent planning and conducting of
a program, is a productive procedure. When we feel we have a
part in planning the program, we accept it as our project and
we respond by helping to make it successful.

    b. We need to learn to accept responsibility. Even though
some of us are willing to be led into a state of dependency, we
also, whether we are aware of it or not, want to do things for
ourselves. We want to express our will, to find an outlet for
our particular talents. All of us are both dependent and independent.

In the Indiana Plan the adult learner helps to determine
the educational program because the Plan recognizes that learning facts alone is not the only kind of learning we are seeking. Subject matter is needed, but we also need to learn how
to use the facts of subject matter through sharing responsibility and better communication.

Responsibility is strongly emphasized as the learner is
gradually introduced into ways of accepting it. We, the learners,
must start at the beginning to learn how to take our share of
the responsibility by having specific things to do. Thus the

61

whole learning group, for instance, takes part in the planning: participants become responsible for the physical set-up, committees of learners investigate and secure resource persons and materials when they are needed, and the learners are involved in establishing the goals and in evaluating the progress. These are a few illustrations of tasks which, with appropriate guidance, will help us to learn by doing. We learn what responsibility means by accepting it, doing the work involved, evaluating the outcome, and trying to do it better.

c. We need to satisfy our personal reasons for learning. Adults may come to a class, discussion group, forum, or similar meeting the first time because someone told them they should be there. But they are not likely to continue unless they feel they are getting something out of it. The more we comprehend in terms of personal meaning, the more intimately we will associate ourselves with the project. Each one of us who feels the desire to know more has personal reasons for wanting to know. Rarely do we pursue learning in religion for learning's sake alone.

This problem of making a religious learning program real to us, of directing it to our personal needs, is both vital and difficult. It is difficult because many of us believe that our problems are unique; "nobody knows the trouble I've seen." To be minutely technical, this is true. But in actual life situations, there is enough of sameness in most of our problems and the way we have handled them so that we can be of real help to one another. We can be of help if we know what some of our mutual learning needs and problems are. We must be willing to spend the time and effort to explore these needs alone and together with our fellow learners.

d. We resist being told what to do. A number of years ago, of two comedians who were in the public favor, one would constantly try to convince the other of a policy which he should adopt or a deed he should perform. The other would reply, "Even if it is good, I wouldn't like it."

In some modified form this is a response with which we must deal in all kinds of adult education. This resistance to some other person's idea exhibits itself most clearly in learning situations which are superimposed on the learner--in which he has very little if anything to say about what goes on. Most of us resist ideas that threaten our right to think and act in the way we have been doing.

Some will wish to boss the program, and some will spend an unwarranted amount of time splitting hairs on issues. Fortunately, only few of us take these extreme attitudes. But these few are often influential. Every one of us, to a degree, resists others' opinions, perhaps for good reasons.

Some of us "know more than anyone else in the group" and feel that what we can learn from such a procedure will be minor or insignificant. Such an attitude is bound to hamper the operation of the whole group unless it can be overcome. These persons must often be allowed to take a considerable role in the planning, but they must be helped to respect the suggestions of others in the group. Proper teamwork on the part of the group can usually reduce this threat to group learning, and gain the balanced participation of all members.

4. How Learners Share in Program Development

a. In terms of needs. We act according to what we consider as our needs. The problems we think are important are the ones we want to work on. But these may not be our real needs. Indeed, we may not be able to recognize our real needs clearly because they are beclouded by symptoms. The needs we express (which might be considered our symptomatic needs and be evidence of real needs) will seem real to us even if they are not our real needs. If we can't understand what our real learning needs are, then those which we can understand become our needs. Adults want to feel that they know what they need even when they don't. But we must work with the knowledge, feelings, and attitudes we have.

During the early meetings of the training group, the participants identify the topics of the educational program they are going to pursue for the next few months. To discover, at this point, what they need to know is very important. If adults feel they are not getting what they think they need, even if this is pretty vaguely defined, they tend to lose interest in the program. The task, then, is to try to discover the real needs common to the persons in the group. By a continuing process of re-examination and refinement we can peel off the layers of symptomatic needs and begin to get our real needs together. This takes time--sometimes months. Because freedom of expression develops slowly, it is essential in volunteer adult groups to allow plenty of time for the group to make these decisions.

As progress is made with this procedure over a period of time, fewer symptomatic needs are dealt with and more real needs appear. This assumes that a constant evaluation of needs takes place.

The minister or the educational director might be able to identify the needs more clearly than members of the group, but until most of the group participants begin to see in the project some direct relationship to what they consider are their needs, they will not completely accept the opinions of the professional leaders.

b. _In terms of interest_. Interest is a vital factor in any program of adult religious education. A volunteer adult learning program cannot begin unless the potential learners are sufficiently interested to make an appearance. What arouses interest is often difficult to identify. Our interests are the factors which prompt us to give attention to the learning situation in spite of other influences and demands for our time. When interests and needs coincide we are motivated toward a productive learning experience.

It will be observed that the reason for our interest most frequently expressed is the "good" that it will do for us. Fortunately, this is more evident at the beginning of an adult learning program such as we are setting up. But the person who is organizing the program has to face reality. If personal concern and selfishness is initially the reason why many of us are motivated to learn, then we must attack on that basis. As a matter of fact, that basis is as good as any. A certain amount of personal concern is healthy and natural. To try to discourage it, even an overabundance of it, during the early stages of a program, is not advisable.

Some of the major reasons why individualists initially join such groups, reasons which we must recognize and deal with are:

(1) Selfishness or an over-concern with what we can get out of it.

(2) Loneliness. We want to be with other people.

(3) Some friend or relative plans to attend the meetings. We like to be with this person so we become interested through him.

(4) Recognition that we really need to know more about our religion and a sincere desire to study and learn.

(5) Trouble in our lives, or what we think is trouble (sickness, want, unhappy relations with others) provides us with a motive to seek out some solution. This may furnish the initial interest.

(6) Social reasons. Some persons will be interested largely because it is the "thing to do," or "the place to go," or because "the right people" will be present.

(7) The daily example set by other persons who may be, or may have been, involved in a learning program.

(8) The fact that the help of the learner is needed often becomes a powerful interest stimulator.

No attempt should be made to classify as "good" or "bad" those ordinary problems and situations which may arouse initial interest. They are listed merely because they are practical reasons we must recognize and deal with.

There are other important interest factors which should be recognized and used by those of us who help start a program of adult religious education. _First_, we must recognize some of the initial interests which make us sufficiently concerned to want to attend a learning program. _Second_, we must help each other as learners to turn those interests to the advantage of the persons in the group. When the program is turned toward the interests of the individual learners, and each one helps to determine the program in terms of his present interests, we have begun a program of learning which will, like symptomatic needs, vary and change. A program which has begun based on the interests of the individual learners at the early stages of our learning together obviously should change as we mature and develop. In order for learners to keep a sustained interest, this change must be allowed for. One way to handle it is to encourage the participants to evaluate their program and to identify the need for a more mature approach to their problems.

Interests which are in evidence at the beginning are often a good starting point for the program. But adult religious programs should progress from this point to the consideration of matters which will help us (a) to improve the way we think and, therefore, (b) to change our behavior willingly and in desirable ways. Sufficient interest must be aroused and maintained, perhaps over a long period, if we are to see the need for improvement, are to want to change, and are to become willing to do something about it.

Many devices can be used to help develop interest and keep it at a level high enough to facilitate learning. We usually think of clever advertising through such media as newspapers, church bulletins, word-of-mouth contacts, posters and direct mail, as devices which will develop an interest in the program. It is true that these may sufficiently stimulate curiosity and bring a number of persons together to learn what is going to happen, but this is only the first step in the program. The next step is vital if the program is to succeed: to get the participants to help determine the substance of the educational program.

By far the most effective interest-holders are those which relate to the needs which we as learners are able to comprehend. Participation, though, is an important interest sustaining factor which serves to stimulate each person and to help him feel that he is needed and that the whole group is served by the sharing of his knowledge and experience.

c. In terms of capacities. That all men are created equal is an idea which can cause misunderstanding and confusion in education when only partly understood. That we are equal before God and under the law and must be allowed equality of opportunity is basic to free people. That we are the same size physically or have the same capacity for learning is, of course, untrue.

Capacity is our potential; it represents what we are capable of learning. Our capabilities are conditioned by a total pattern of causes -- some hereditary and some environmental. In other words, our learning potential is determined partly by our inheritance and partly by the various circumstances which have shaped our lives up to this moment. For the great majority of us, however, our capacity for learning is tremendous in comparison with the use we make of it.

Almost everyone can learn new ideas at any age and has a tremendous untapped capacity for learning. The use we have made of our capacities in great part accounts for our differences, for no two persons make use of their capacities in the same way or to the same extent. Each of us is a unique person whose problems of development differ from those of others, and each of us is trying in his own separate way to achieve a measure of satisfaction.

67

With all these differences in capabilities and utilization of abilities it might appear that learning together would be impossible. Actually we are able to make great strides in learning in free and purposeful church groups, but a degree of common ground must be found in order to start a successful program. In learning groups the common denominator, or enough sameness so the group can get started, can generally be arrived at by the participants themselves.

When the group participants exercise their freedom under a moderate amount of guidance, they adjust to and compensate for these noted differences. Each person, regardless of his background, his experience, or his schooling can, and frequently does, bring to the group a fresh and unique viewpoint. Instead of causing the program to be geared to the individual whose development is considered most inadequate, the differences among individuals in a learning group should constitute its basic strength. The ideas of the "inadequates" may be as helpful as those of the others. We provide an opportunity for persons of differing capabilites to retain their individuality because of the differences which exist, yet work with different persons in an area of sameness.

SECTION E

VOLUNTARY LEARNING ACTIVITIES

1. Introduction

A "voluntary learning activity" is a term which we might easily misunderstand. Actually it does imply a force of some kind to bring about action. It is the source of that force and how it operates that is important. Force will be present in one form or another in every situation where people are together. It either comes from each one of us as we extend considerable control over ourselves through self-discipline (internal) or it will be placed on us by others (external).

People can be lined up, given shovels and forced by others to learn to dig their own graves by digging them. So, too, they can be forced to learn for fear of losing social standing, jobs, etc. Sometimes people have been forced to dig their intellectual and spiritual graves by those of us who feel we know what's good for people. We can help destroy real initiative in the learners, causing their deterioration as free individuals.

There are probably few of us who haven't heard a group in control in a church, industry, labor union, or school, trying to discover how they can put something over to their people, as if they weren't part of the people. Usually some person in the group will point out with a knowing smile that there are ways in which this or that can be accomplished. Indeed there are ways -- all the way from the bayonet to complete individualism.

No activity or movement fails to find a leader of some sort. Someone always feels that "it won't be done or done right if I don't do it." In a properly functioning group every participant accepts this challenge, thus preventing the emergence of a dominating leader or clique. And of greater significance, through such activities we begin to extend our development of self-discipline, which is the kind of force we need to promote voluntary learning activities. As we recognize we are responsible for the program -- that its success or failure is very much in our hands -- we tend voluntarily to extend ourselves to make the program succeed. When the pressure to learn is from within us, based on a disciplined free will and a personal reason for learning, we are well on our way toward a successful adventure in learning.

To know how to make more mature decisions voluntarily is one of our major learning tasks. It is an individual job. And it would seem difficult to learn the meaning of freedom and release from fear when being forced to learn it. It's very much like saying we're going to make you free if we have to throw you in jail to do it. Voluntary adult learning is indeed in keeping with our great gift of free choice. We can accept God's grace or reject it. So we can accept or reject the opportunity to learn more about how to relate ourselves to God.

This, of course, does not mean that those who are concerned with organizing religious programs should make no effort until people come forward and say "I want to learn." When this request is widely made it will be a greater day for civilization than this one. Potential learners must be confronted with a vital, interesting, and productive program of learning in which they can cooperatively use their talents and time. No guarantees, no misrepresentations, no pat formulae, no ideal procedure for all learning occasions, but no under-statements either. People must have an opportunity to make a decision.

2. The Potential Learner Makes
   a Voluntary Decision

Finally, it is the potential learner who decides. His decision, to be sure, may be selfishly motivated: "What am I going to get out of it?" Regardless of how the idealist deplores this attitude, it is still a dominant force. Unless the program produces results that give the adult learner something he thinks he can use, the program will fail. The adult participants not only decide whether or not they want to start such an activity but also decide its life span.

3. Why A Voluntary Learning Activity is Desirable

   a. Nobody can learn for us. In a voluntary adult learning activity we realize more fully that people can be taught but not "learned." A leader or teacher can help us to feel right about a learning situation; he can't feel for us. Neither can he "learn" us, although many times we approach the learner as if we can.

The following ideas and practices, which exist in some teaching situations, indicate that we often seem to ignore the fact

70

that learning is very personal and that all of it must take place within the learner.

(1) The notion that since resistance to new ideas and situations is ever present in all of us, it is good to make learners "mad" because then they'll really learn. We do learn something when we're angry, but it's not the kind of learning that helps us to exercise self-discipline and advance toward maturity.

(2) The threat, if you don't "get your lesson" some sort of unfortunate situation will occur. You'll be embarrassed by the teacher or leader or some "smarter" people in the group. You won't be able to make an appropriate remark at the proper time, and this will create tension in you that you will remember and correct. Adults certainly will remember the embarrassment. They will often correct it by not coming back for more.

(3) Another idea is that people come to meetings of an educational nature because they lack knowledge. The amount of knowledge they have is a matter of degree, but every person brings some knowledge to a learning group. Sometimes we can't express what we do know. But teachers should not assume that learners are completely ignorant. Our experiences and knowledge that we have and could make use of in further learning may be badly disorganized. And we probably lack much specific information. But it is easier for a teacher to know what we need to know if he goes through the learning process _with_ us instead of attempting to provide it wholly _for_ us.

(4) Overdependence on packaged programs. Unless there is a flexible program adapted to the needs which are recognized by the particular group, we can't take full advantage of all the learning which could take place. It may be true that we should know what the packaged lesson or lecture contains. But the leader can't know how the information transmitted is received unless he consults the receiver. He can't always tell by the expression on our faces during the transmitting process.

We can tell, however, when the needed parts of the package are adapted to our needs when we learners do part of the adapting.

Many indications show that we work at the process of adult religious education as if the learner can be "learned." Certainly we know better, but our actions belie our words. Tension, fear, pat and rigid procedures, and authoritarian techniques which maintain a solid wall between the learner and the teacher or leader have no rightful place in adult religious education. If we are agreed that people can't be "learned," the next step is to forthrightly discontinue methods of learning which point in that direction.

b. <u>Each person comes into a personal relationship with God</u>. Our relationship with God is a personal one which we must finally discover by ourselves. Surely we can help each other in the process. Prayer, corporate and private worship, study and discussion can all help to reveal and enlighten. But we bring meaning out of all of this in terms of our personal ability to understand. And we understand what is meaningful to us, not what others think ought to be meaningful to us.

Our relationship with God is as real as we wish to make it. In this sense it is voluntary. God does not force us, but rather offers us opportunities. The relationship is personal; the process of attaining is voluntary. It is essential that a learning program which helps to provide the fuel for understanding how constantly to improve this voluntary relationship be also voluntary.

c. <u>We select and attend the church of our choice</u>. The church is a voluntary institution. In many places in this world we can select the church we wish to attend. It is our choice to make. There may be various reasons why it is difficult to make a voluntary selection, but nevertheless we cannot be forced to attend church, and many people don't. Our relationship with the church and with the educational programs the church promotes is voluntary.

72

4. How Is the Indiana Plan
a Voluntary Experience?

This educational idea supports the notion that force is an agent that does not contribute to the kind of learning needed to develop mature insights. The voluntary nature of the program exhibits itself in two areas; attendance and participation.

a. __Attendance.__ The educational programs can be made interesting enough that some people will voluntarily substitute learning together about themselves and their religion for some of the other activities which have kept them so busy before. Voluntary attendance can be stimulated by:

(1) Intelligent selling of the enterprise at the start of the program. Loose, thoughtless sales talks often mean that we find after attending that we aren't getting what we bargained for, or think we should get. We either quit or attend poorly.

(2) Comfortable meeting places.

(3) Proper educational facilities (blackboards, good lights, tables, chairs, movie equipment).

(4) Good resources (resource material -- books, films, pamphlets, recordings, etc.), and resource persons -- men and women who are well versed in subject areas being covered and able to serve appropriately as resource persons.

(5) Effective leadership and group participation. If the leaders and the group participants are trained together to participate actively as a learning team, interest tends to be maintained.

(6) Programs based on needs as the participants understand those needs.

(7) Helping participants feel it is their program; encouraging volunteers to assume specific responsibilities (such as arranging the meeting place, investigating and providing resource materials, getting appropriate resource persons, getting and operating slide projectors, serving as leader, etc.)

In no case, however, should a record of attendance be kept in order to keep a check on specific persons. We should attend to learn about our religion not to answer roll calls, fill out forms, and bow to the machinery of operation. We must guard against becoming "operators" who substitute the process for the goal.

b. _Participation_. For a successful program it is necessary that as many as possible become involved by their own desire to do so. We all know that some people will not step up and say, "I'll do it!" But when we are all trained to participate even some of the meekest will begin to share their part of this task when they see it is in the order of things; that many others are doing it; that it's not as difficult as it seemed. A few members will never volunteer to serve as leader, and we should not try to force them. It is well not to direct too much time and attention to those who don't feel they want to get up before the group. Some of us have to be brought along gradually. Some of us are reluctant to assume personal responsibility for the program through active oral participation and the acceptance of the numerous jobs to be done in the mechanical phases of the program. If we exert too much pressure on those who are reluctant to participate actively in various ways, we can make the problem worse so that sometimes these persons will leave the program.

SECTION F

FORMAL AND INFORMAL EDUCATIONAL PROCEDURES

1. Introduction

The task of re-examining our present ideas and adding to our knowledge can be accomplished in many ways or combinations of ways: talking with our friends, counseling with our minister, reading and private study, attendance at courses and programs given by the churches and the schools, pursuing hobbies of various kinds, listening to some radio programs, listening to and watching some TV programs, and having family discussions.

Some of these ways of learning are called formal, others informal. The lines of distinction between these two "kinds" of
education are often drawn too finely. We are all prone to want
to take sides and to be "for" this and "against" that way of
learning. Here we should recognize that our goal is not to
support or reject a kind of education. Our goal stands clearly
before us: to learn better how to know and serve God.

We use different kinds of procedures as means to help us
reach the goal. If these devices seem to help us accomplish
our goal we use them; if not, we discard them. In the Indiana
Plan it has been discovered that formal approaches such as the
sermon, the lecture, the speech, and the symposium have been
effective for certain purposes. Also semi-formal approaches
such as the various kinds of forums have proven useful. All
groups have used group discussion as the core of the program to
offer initial training in leadership and group participation.
As the program broadens into a long-range vehicle, they have
used the various educational procedures most appropriate for
other purposes to accomplish the goal of adult religious education.

2. Both Kinds Are Needed

Actually the nature of the Indiana Plan precludes the arbitrary
classification of various procedures as better than others.
The program is highly flexible and is designed to meet the particular need of the church group at a particular time. Sometimes one procedure is found to be effective, sometimes another,
depending upon the problems at hand. The people within each
church will differ in their interests, abilities, and attitudes,
and in the problems and needs they recognize--all factors must
be taken into account in an educational program. A good example of how we try to avoid facing up to the real learning
problems which beset us is often the desire to have every program a Bible study group. History, dates, biblical personalities, and verses are studied and memorized. A few will say we
really had a good program.

"Why was the program good?" questioned a clergyman.

"Because it is the Word. And you can never know enough about it," replied the chairman of the program.

"Do we know about the Bible by learning names, dates, and verses?"

"How else can we learn the Bible?" asked the program chairman.

These remarks are not universal. But they are made often enough to be a serious deterrent to meaningful programs of adult religious education. We often try to oversimplify programs by standardizing them.

When we discover together what some of our problems are, and then use the Bible for the great resource book it is, it speaks to those problems. The Bible speaks in a universal language. We can learn what it has to say in terms of the needs and problems which we recognize. In the Indiana Plan, adult programs **are** not conducted to **validate the Bible. Qualified resource persons** and **authoritative materials** do this. **In** this Plan people often meet together to learn the significance of the Bible as it speaks to their problems. The best group learning procedure to use in a given situation will depend upon the nature of the problems, the learners involved, the goals of the program, and the resources available.

Adult religious education cannot be successfully standardized because people aren't standardized. The lessons in the Bible regarding God and our behavior toward Him and our fellowmen are universal. But for us to see their universal scope and truths in personal terms is the hub of the problem. Sometimes we must go about it in different ways because of our different experiences, abilities, and all that go to make us unique personalities. Differences which exist, then, can be turned to the real values. When we recognize that these differences exist, we more carefully analyze the needs of all of us who are engaged in a new experience of learning together. We begin to discover meaning in the process of seeking God together and individually in various ways.

3. Formal and Informal Education Distinguished

Attempts to distinguish between formal and informal education by careful definition for our use is difficult. It should be recognized that a distinction should be made between formal and informal education, and formal and informal ways of making education possible. Formal education according to Dictionary of Education[3] is "(1) any training or education that is conventional, given in an orderly, logical, planned, and systematic manner; thus formal education is said to end with school attendance ; (2) in a derogatory sense, any educational program that is confined to the experiences of the students within the classroom itself, failing to make use of the student's incidental and varied experiences outside the classroom."

Informal education allows the learner in varying degrees to participate to the extent that he can clarify, assimilate and make meaningful, on the spot, the information and ideas being treated. Group discussions, seminars, and various kinds of forums are often referred to as informal. Because the Indiana Plan is based on situations and needs at a particular time with a unique group of persons, it endorses and uses the educational procedures which seem best to help participants to reach the educational goals of a given meeting.

4. Formal and Informal Characteristics

The purpose here is to present a few characteristics often associated with the words formal and informal education in order to become better acquainted with those terms. No attempt is made here to judge any of these characteristics as "good" or "bad."

a. Characteristics of formal adult education

(1) The students are usually thought of as an audience and they listen. Their task is to learn what is presented. They are not often called upon to speak.

(2) The lecture or sermon often is a predominant feature.

---

[3]Carter V. Good, editor, Dictionary of Education (New York: McGraw-Hill, 1945).

(3) Programs are usually prepared for the learners by others.

(4) In religious and secular education the word class is associated with formal activities -- a teacher and a group of pupils who meet regularly at a particular time and place.

(5) The word school is frequently used in formal educational activities (e.g., church schools, Sunday school, high school).

(6) Credit or some sort of tangible reward is closely allied with formal educational activities in secular education. So many points or hours of credit are given for the satisfactory completion of an area of study. Credit also means the certification of the completion of a course of study.

(7) Course is a vital word in formal education. The educational program is usually arranged around courses or established limited subject areas in which instruction is given.

(8) Subject as used in formal education means a particular field of organized knowledge -- like mathematics or English.

(9) The teacher is the "boss."

(10) The program is conducted over a specified period of time.

(11) Examinations, or tests, are usually given periodically to determine whether the student can satisfactorily recall and organize, usually in written form, the information that has been transmitted to him in a course.

(12) The teacher's evaluation of the student is of great importance.

(13) The students usually compete.

b. Characteristics of organized informal adult education.

(1) Great flexibility and variety in procedures and resources are used.

(2) The teacher or leader acts as a catalyst, a stimulator, a helper, a guide, a coordinator. He is not the "boss."

(3) Each individual is a teacher-learner.

(4) Direct participation by all, or as many persons as possible, is vital.

(5) Sharing ideas, experiences, and information by all persons involved is necessary.

(6) The content is based on problems and needs expressed by those who are involved.

(7) Subject materials are a means, not the end.

(8) Some informal education might be called incidental education.

(9) We become involved because there is a demand or need put upon us by ourselves. Our goal is to satisfy that demand or need, not to get a grade.

(10) To an increasing degree the participants determine the content, process, procedures, and resources.

(11) The participants' evaluation is of great importance.

SECTION G

OUTWARD GROWTH

1. Introduction

One significant characteristic of the Indiana Plan for Adult Education is that, to be effective, it must be an ever-expanding, outward-moving series of experiences. It is designed to accomplish this. We learn to accept a degree of personal responsibility for our own growth and for that of our fellow learners in order to use them as means of relating ourselves to God and to other persons through mutual educational experiences. Outward growth feeds on sharing. It withers in a purely competitive atmosphere.

2. Toward Corporate Understanding

In this Plan great emphasis is placed on making our new learning more meaningful by using our new insights in outward-moving service to others.

a. At the outset of the program we meet for several sessions of concentrated training. This helps to provide a framework in which we can learn to work together, to identify and provide some of our real learning needs, to learn about ourselves as learners, to plan better, to talk more to the point, to locate resource persons and materials, to use listening as a learning tool, to set and stick to a goal and to conduct a careful evaluation. We also learn to deal with religious teachings as program content.

b. Next, we extend ourselves in other groups or organizations within the church in two ways: (1) we try to interest more persons in a productive learning experience by suggesting that they become involved in some training and learning activities provided by this adult education plan; (2) we use our talents and new insights in the other groups or organizations to which we may belong in the church.

c. But this is not enough. The Plan is not really successful until the church is in the community as a living, vital, dynamic organism -- an organism which provides the climate in which a Christian society flourishes. This Christian atmosphere is provided by all of us in our everyday relationship with every person we meet. The real expansion, the productive outward growth, comes when we use what we have learned and take a more active and intelligent part in the affairs of our church, and then bring the church into the community. We become concerned and active in political affairs, economic situations, Boy and Girl Scouts, Red Cross, Community Chest, health drives, and such other community affairs whose goals are to serve God through people. Those who learn the full meaning of corporateness by studying and talking about it, and then by practicing it in service to everyone, are moving outward.

The whole human family is large, and it takes expansive ideas to encompass it. Here, of course, we must guard against substituting fanciful thoughts and good feelings for meaningful action and service. We can hold interesting meetings about the plight of the aborigines and be unfit to live within our immediate family. We learn how to move outward by starting with a healthy look at ourselves, then moving outward through the family, the church, and into the community. The church is then in action among us all.

3. Our Ego-Centered Nature

The starting phase of the continuing process of learning includes sharing, accepting, and helping (giving, taking and doing). In this phase we can learn more about ourselves and other people and how to behave toward them in order to understand and help them. But there are forces which operate against this desired end. One such deterrent is preoccupation with "self."

We all seem to be overly concerned about ourselves and not concerned enough about other people. Now, self-centeredness can impede learning and interfere with our spiritual and mental development as creative human beings. Withdrawing within ourselves through selfishness inhibits the insights necessary to become more mature persons -- i.e., persons who move from self-centeredness toward a God-centered life, which is the important part of a person's life that is related to God through other people. " . . . as you did it not to one of the least of these, you did it not to me." (Matthew 25:45)

We cannot for long isolate ourselves from others and remain whole -- healthy, balanced persons. "If anyone says 'I love God' and hates his brother, he is a liar. . . ." (I John 4:20) Too much "looking out for ourselves" is a malignancy which upsets this balance. Thinking about our lives becomes so important to us and takes so much time that we begin to crowd out everything else but us. Eventually we destroy ourselves, because we have cut off a source of learning and growing when we have denied ourselves the values of association. If we do not try to relate ourselves to others we can't understand them; consequently, others become of little help to us in learning.

81

Therefore, if we are to experience the satisfaction of purposeful learning and growing together, we are bound to recognize at once the pitfalls of excessive self-love (egoism). At the same time, we ought not to ignore the need for self-esteem.

The irony of the notion which many of us share that we must "look out for ourselves or no one else will" is that we live together and we cannot isolate ourselves as individuals from the stream of life about us; we are in that stream. The more we look out for ourselves, the more we separate ourselves from others. Our task, then, is to learn to be a responsible person, preserving a degree of independence, through self-awareness and self-esteem, all the while recognizing our dependence on God and upon other people. "For as in one body we have many members, and all the members do not have the same function, so we, though many, are one body in Christ, and individually members one of another. Having gifts that differ according to the grace given to us, let us use them. . . ." (Romans 12:4-6)

We have to deal with several problems in our journey toward learning how to know God better and how best to serve Him. Our outward movement toward thoughtful service to the whole of society is a positive step in this journey. To take this step we must bring into a workable relationship the self-centered characteristics of our nature and the social-centered aspects of it. Rather than worry about whether or not self-centeredness is bad or good, let us first recognize what it is, and how it can be used to serve rather than enslave us.

Self-centeredness may, indeed, serve a good purpose. It is a sort of built-in protective device. But good, clean drinking water also serves a purpose. We only need so much of it, however. So with self-centeredness. But we must be aware of ourselves -- our limitations, our talents. We must know and accept ourselves for what we are and what we are trying to become. A degree of self-esteem is essential if we are to move outward toward a greater social-centered life.

Early in this learning experience we begin to discover as best we can what our real (as opposed to "imagined") self is like. Armed with this new discovery, we may gradually learn how to relate to others in the group, as we become acquainted with their problems, needs, aspirations, and concerns.

We resist, to some extent, learning how to give a fuller, more disciplined expression to our wills by giving more of ourselves to our co-learners. This attempt to break out of our ego-centeredness hurts because it reveals to us, and to others, parts of ourselves which are not always pleasant to us or to others. But this revelation or self-examining can help us discover our own blocks to learning.

4. Self-Examination

Fruitful self-examination can be accomplished alone or in groups, but always it must have an adequate frame of reference. In the Indiana Plan participants examine themselves in terms of:

a. How I work with other members of the learning team. Here the individual has a chance to face himself in terms of the corporate body -- people present in the learning group, not others 10,000 miles away in a sort of dream world. We learn how to work with others when we deal with the problem in a face-to-face, practical situation in our learning group.

How and why do I resist certain ideas and personalities? Is this resistance justifiable?

How and why do I cooperate?

Do I help those I like and ignore those I dislike?

How and why do I contribute to the enterprise?

Do I try to dominate others? If so, how? Why?

b. What have I been doing with the things I have learned or with what I am trying to learn?

Some dangers of corrosive self-examination should be carefully noted:

-- Over-emphasis on examination of psychological motives, with which the average learner is not capable of dealing.

-- Attempting to classify ourselves and others in neat psychological compartments.

-- Undue concern about process (the educational procedure used and what happened to us when that procedure was used) at the expense of content (the subject matter under consideration and what was said about it). These two aspects of learning must be treated in the light of their relative importance.

Sincere self-examination with the help of fellow-learners helps us immensely to move outward into a dynamic program. It will go far toward removing significant barriers to our educational progress. By it we recognize more about what we are, and we accept ourselves and others as persons struggling to learn to live and grow together.

A combination of several valuable approaches has been found helpful in discovering what hinders us from transferring some of our self-love into service to others.

-- Private prayer and meditation can help us to relate ourselves more intimately with God. Through this growing relationship we may discover a great deal about ourselves and our duties toward His whole family.

-- In our educational group meetings we should be concerned not only with subject matter but also with ways we can actively relate ourselves to the ultimate goal of adult religious education: to learn more about how to know God better in order to better serve Him. We accomplish a large part of this goal through our fellow humans, " . . . for he who does not love his brother whom he has seen, cannot love God whom he has not seen." (I John 4:20)

5. Moving Out

As we learn to deal with ourselves we can overcome some of the restrictions which too much self-concern has imposed on us. Then we become more a working part of the corporate body -- all of humanity.

But we don't move into this relationship at once. It is perhaps never fully realized by most of us, but we can move toward that goal. This moving toward the goal can be illustrated with a series of concentric circles:

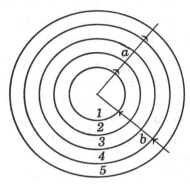

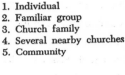

1. Individual
2. Familiar group
3. Church family
4. Several nearby churches
5. Community

The inside circle (1) represents the individual; the next circle (2) represents a familiar group; the third circle (3), the particular church with which the individual is involved; the fourth circle (4) represents several nearby churches of the same communion; and the outside circle (5), the whole human community.

If we are to develop and grow by association with others we must, in a sense, break out of ourselves as represented by the inner circle into a larger group of persons. We have probably accomplished this in our own family relationships and to some degree in groups outside the family. But mere incidental association with other human beings (such as in some "fellowship" meetings) does not necessarily provide the substance through which learning takes place. We can feel quite alone in a crowd.

In order to establish a climate that helps us to feel right about fellow-learners, we start slowly -- in a familiar group

(Circle 2). This group, in the Indiana Plan, is the ten or fifteen persons who start the adult educational program or make up a training group. But this group must become more than a group of cold, impersonal, or highly critical people if they are to lower some of their defenses and create an atmosphere conducive to learning. In this familiar group (Circle 2), among other things, we can learn about ourselves and about each other-- and to help one another in our learning activities.

The next step in the outward movement is into Circle 3, a wider circle in the congregation. By this time some of us have learned some educational skills and insights and more about ourselves and others. We can now be of greater service to the church by practicing these skills in service to the whole church.[4] We can develop broader educational programs which involve persons from a number of organizations. Part of these educational programs at this stage of moving outward, should involve real efforts to help persons in the whole church to become acquainted with one another on more than a handshake or smile-and-nod-basis.

There is a real need for the type of educational activity that stimulates the congregation, or large segments of it, to work together regularly and purposefully as a body, or family. This type of educational activity does not exist in many congregations. It is not achieved simply through appeals for cooperation. People have to see reasons and have a purpose. The Indiana Plan provides soundly, but slowly, the foundation upon which this broader relationship can be built.

But we don't stop here. At this point the flower is only partly in bloom. Step 4 in this dynamic process involves interchurch meetings. Those of us in the same communion who live in towns close by, and also have a similar adult education program, meet together occasionally. Ten or fifteen persons from each of four or five nearby churches meet once or twice a year

---

[4]Chapter III describes briefly the broadening of the program.

to compare notes about their respective educational programs or to conduct an educational program of mutual concern. This is another opportunity to widen our horizons; to broaden our outlook. By and large, many of us isolate ourselves in our own town and our own church in that town, and our own group in that church, and our own self in that group. The Indiana Plan tends to reverse this tendency toward isolation.

As in any effective learning process we must approach the goal gradually, step-by-step. Through the steps described up to this point we may approach our ultimate goal: to know God better so that we can better serve Him.

The last step in our educational journey is a vital one. It is not easy even if we have approached it gradually. It can and must be accomplished.

Circle 5 represents our service to God through the whole human community. We have learned in small groups. We have expanded in other organizations in our church, and with other churches. Now we practice our stewardship with everyone regardless of their creed or color or nationality. We work as laborers. We extend ourselves not as academic observers of humanity, but as doers, as persons who feel we are part of humanity. The Indiana Plan is designed to help us learn to work. At this point we have the opportunity to use our learning in Christian service in a broad field; we practice our vocation everywhere within reach.

CHAPTER III

A PATTERN OF ACTION FOR THE INDIANA PLAN

A. <u>INTRODUCTION</u>

The Indiana Plan for Adult Religious Education is a flexible approach to some of the problems of adult religious education in local churches. It is not a panacea or a way of revolutionizing the educational program of a church. It is, however, a tested framework of training and action within which an effective adult program can evolve. It must be adapted to the unique characteristics of the local situation, and its successful development requires the sincere cooperation of a clergyman who has rapport with his congregation.

The whole plan is intended as a vehicle which people can use to get at a major educational goal of the church: to help us grow in our understanding of God so that we can better serve Him. To help people strive toward this goal, the Indiana Plan aims at three things:

1. To stimulate adults to RECOGNIZE that some of their religious education needs can be met through educational programs in which they share responsibility and explore their relationship with God, other persons, and themselves.

2. To assist lay people to ACCEPT a share of responsibility for devising and conducting educational programs to meet the religious educational needs they can recognize.

3. To encourage people to USE their religious educational opportunities to understand basic Christian doctrines and to interpret their talents actively through the church and the whole human community.

The Indiana Plan develops in any church through three phases which we might describe as (1) Starting the Plan, (2) Expanding the Plan, (3) Consolidating the Plan. The way in which these phases develop and the length of time required to develop them depend largely upon the unique nature of the local church. Our main purpose here is to describe briefly, and in general terms, (a) the characteristic activities of these three phases and (b) their purposes.

B. STARTING THE PLAN

The first step in starting this Plan in a local church is to enlist the cooperation of the clergyman. The person who is to help guide the development of the Plan in the church, called "the trainer" (see Chapter II, Section A, and Chapter V, Section C), must make sure that the clergyman understands and approves the Plan. His cooperation and the encouragement which he can impart to the participants during the development of the program are key factors of success.

Next, the trainer and the clergyman, in a preliminary planning session, adapt the Plan to the local church problems and needs insofar as this is possible at the outset. One question at this point is: Who should help start the Plan? At least one training group of from 10 to 15 persons is desirable. It is generally best (but not absolutely necessary) to start with people of both sexes and various ages. For example, "starting groups" have been composed of (a) representatives of all church organizations and committees, (b) members of a women's organization, (c) a group of Sunday school teachers, (d) a number of interested adults, (e) a group of people who had been meeting as a study group.

While it is advantageous to offer the program to everyone in the congregation at the start, it is not always feasible or possible to do so. Since the membership of the early training groups will affect the way in which the program later expands in the church, it is important to include at the start those persons who might become the most successful agents of expansion. It should be stressed here, however, that this program is not beamed to the so-called "well-read" church members. It is most important to start with participants who are willing to try to learn together.

The first meeting of the participants is usually a preliminary session at which the trainer explains the Indiana
Plan -- its aims, procedures, and possible results. The next
step in the developing program is usually a series of 2 to 4
weekly or semi-weekly two-hour meetings designed to give the
group preliminary participation training through the use of
group discussion. This group learning procedure[1] is described
and demonstrated by the trainer and volunteer participants
together so that participants can actually begin to identify
and develop leadership and group participation skills necessary
for effective teamwork. During these sessions, the topics of
discussion are of lesser importance, the emphasis being on
everyone's learning to know and accept the duties of responsible participation.

Usually by the fourth meeting, a training group is ready
to begin planning and conducting full-length discussions (of
1 to 1 1/2 hours) on topics determined by the participants themselves. In general, they are usually either religious teachings
that participants can relate readily to everyday living or problems of everyday living on which religious teachings can be
brought to bear. The participants set realistic goals, obtain
appropriate resource materials and conduct their own weekly or
biweekly discussions, with the assistance of the trainer. The
clergyman can serve as subject authority, or resource person,
clarifying questions and providing information when professional
assistance is needed in appropriate subject areas. The trainer
continues to assist the participants to become an effective
learning team.

How many full-length practice sessions are needed? There
is no definite answer. The participants are setting out to
become a creative learning team, a team of persons able to identify some common educational needs and to help each other meet
those needs through discussing religious teachings in terms of

---
[1]See *Participation Training for Adult Education* (Bethany
Press, 1965), by Paul Bergevin and John McKinley.

its daily significance. They must also learn to accept the responsibilities of developing the inter-personal relationships that make teamwork possible. Usually this is accomplished to some extent in from 10 to 15 full-length discussions.

The participants naturally become greatly interested in the subject, or content, of these discussions. The trainer's job is to keep the participants aware of three reasons for having training in group discussion.

First of all, group discussion is one technique which people can use to explore certain religious teachings, or what they consider subject-matter needs. Through discussion they can learn how vitally important it is to relate information to their experience. The participants find that jargon -- and indeed all information -- must be translated into terms that mean something to them, and that they, the learners, can and must share the responsibility of making information meaningful in personal terms.

Secondly, the discussion group is a convenient small-scale laboratory in which participants can have actual guided experiences with some of the common problems of religious education: developing freedom of expression, developing skills of responsible leadership and group participation, setting clear goals, evaluating, relating information to experience, improving inter-personal communication. These problems are common to both a discussion group and a whole congregation. In the training group they can be clearly recognized and effectively dealt with over a period of time. And the skills and understandings which participants develop through actual experience with these problems lead naturally to their wider application in other educational activities in the church -- which is one reason for expanding the Indiana Plan. The participants grow in these skills and basic educational understandings as the trainer constantly keeps them aware of the problems they are overcoming and helps them to evaluate their teamwork at the end of each session.

The third reason why this Plan begins with participation training through group discussion is less easy to explain but is, nevertheless, of great importance. A church training-discussion group has a special significance: it is a segment of the larger congregational family; thus it is an opportunity for participants to establish and discuss frankly their actual human relationships in the group as individual members of the corporate body.

In the domestic family circle some of us at times discuss openly the self-centeredness, acceptance, rejection, hostility, and cooperation that occur so that we can improve our joint efforts and understand each other better as persons. These same kinds of feelings we have in our church groups, and they affect how we work with our co-learners. Our feelings about our fellow learners affect how we learn and what we learn in the church. But in the church family we do not customarily examine together the way we work toward our common goals, or even what the goals are. The whole congregational family is often too large to exist as a "familiar" group. Although fellowship meetings are usually meant to foster the family-of-God feeling, these meetings do not guide us purposefully to examine our relationships and how we do, and should, work together in God's family. It seems to be assumed that each person automatically takes these matters into consideration privately, or that such consideration is not needed, since God handles these embarrassing details for us.

The discussion training group becomes a familiar group in which participants can explore these vital relationships. Talking about them during the evaluation period after each discussion is natural and inevitable, since these human relationships affect the way in which the participants develop as a learning team.

When the members of the training group have become a creative learning team, they are ready to interrupt this starting phase of their learning venture, at least temporarily, and to help project the program into wider circles of their church. (For a description of the signs of maturing in a starting group, see Chapter IV, Section B).

C. EXPANDING THE PLAN

In brief, the Plan expands as participants use, in the broader life of the church, those insights and skills which they have developed in the discussion training group and in the related activities that characterize expansion. Expansion is characterized by participants moving outward:[2] arousing the interest of other persons in the church and drawing them into new relationships through educational endeavors, accepting new responsibilities, trying to improve and develop needed educational opportunities in the church. Expansion is not exclusively a quantitative process of drawing larger numbers of persons into discussion groups. Expansion involves both quantity and quality. Take, for example, a church of 200 people of whom 15 are engaged in a training group of the Indiana Plan. Expansion would not necessarily consist of immediately drawing 12 or 15 more persons into another training group. Instead it might take the form of helping to improve the church library, or the Lenten program, or the adult Sunday school, or the educational programs for parents of Sunday school children. Ultimately, however, others must be drawn into training in group participation if the plan is to have optimum effect.

There are three basic reasons for expanding the Plan in a church. First, the participants need to extend themselves in service beyond the participation training group. If the participants do not move the program outward, it will die as an exclusive, self-centered study group activity. They must consciously relate themselves to more persons in the congregational-family through the accepting-sharing-helping relationship which they have developed in the training group. This relationship, vital

_____

[2]See Chapter II, Section G, "Outward Growth," for a treatment of the significance of outward movement.

to any Christian family, can be nurtured in educational programs which provide for its development. One purpose of expansion, then, is to provide opportunities in which the trained participants and other parishioners can meet together and begin to develop this accepting-sharing-helping relationship by actively participating in cooperative educational activities.

A second reason for expanding the Plan is that a maximum number of persons in each congregation need training in group participation. They need to learn how to learn together, and a training group is one way to do so. The Indiana Plan is aimed at all the learners in the congregation, not just learners who are leaders. There is no effective short cut that enables a few trained leaders and participants to accomplish educational miracles in a church. We become responsible learners as we actually share experiences, discover our obstacles, and identify our needs in small (training) groups in which responsible, active participation and evaluation are accepted group standards. Therefore, the second main purpose of expansion is to draw an increasing number of persons into participation training groups. This is accomplished often when a training group arouses people's interest through the sponsoring of a variety of planned, large-scale educational programs which offer them opportunities to learn about problems and topics which they consider important.

A third reason for expanding the program is the fact that most churches either (1) have existing educational activities that could be made more effective as educational experiences or (2) lack certain kinds of educational programs which parishioners see a need for. So another main purpose of expansion is to improve existing educational activities in the church and to develop needed ones.

Many local church educational problems and needs can be dealt with as projects by trained participants and by other interested persons in the congregation. Such projects make it necessary that several people learn how to plan effective programs

and how to use various appropriate resources and learning procedures. Thus a secondary purpose of expansion is to train a
growing number of persons in the local church to use educational
tools that are most appropriate to the various educational tasks
that exist in the church.

The program expands in two ways: (a) through individual
efforts and (b) through planned educational activities. In one
respect it expands through individual efforts of participants
as they mediate its influence into the life of the local church
and the community. This kind of expansion goes on almost from
the start as participants develop new educational concepts and
participation skills and gain new insights into their relationship with others and use them in the organized life of the church.
A few individuals can, for instance, exert a positive influence
merely by leading organizations to clarify goals, evaluate their
activities, and plan and conduct programs that explore common
problems and needs which people recognize privately but often
hesitate to suggest as a subject of group study.

The second and more direct way of expanding the program is
through educational activities, planned and sponsored by a training group, in which an increasing number of persons try to understand cooperatively how they relate to God, to each other, and
to themselves.

Often the first step in planned expansion takes place when
the training group and the clergyman meet as an informal survey
group to identify the adult educational problems and needs of
their church. (Usually the participants previously conduct an
informal survey of other members of the congregation.) A list
of these problems and needs usually includes suggestions both
(a) for improving the process of existing adult activities and
(b) for exploring new subjects in either existing activities
or needed activities. Many of the identified needs cannot be
dealt with by a provisional training group because they lie
beyond its jurisdiction. But these needs are at least brought

into the open and can be referred to the proper authority. (For example, improving the educational programs of a men's or women's organization is the responsibility of its members.) Some of the needs that appear on the list can often be handled by one or two persons who wish to volunteer their services and seek out others to help them (sponsoring young adult activities, or organizing visitation teams to welcome new members, or cataloging and publicizing the church library, etc.).

The next step in a typical situation is to choose from the list one educational need which the group can help meet through planning and conducting one or more larger-group educational programs (involving more than 10 or 15 people meeting as a discussion group). Care is taken to avoid conflict with the responsibilities of church administrators and official church committees who may be carrying on established educational work in the church.

Next the trainer guides the training group in planning these meetings carefully: this is his opportunity to teach the participants (a) effective procedures of program planning and (b) how to select and adapt learning procedures for different kinds of educational activities. Three to five planning sessions are usually required. It is a natural learn-by-doing situation. The execution of these programs usually accomplishes three things: (1) it arouses the interest of persons in the church who may as a result be drawn into a training group; (2) it begins to broaden the program in the church by meeting educational needs for more people; (3) it gives trained participants an opportunity to learn how to plan and evaluate different kinds of educational programs.

The actual situations or needs through which planned expansion takes place are unique to the local situation. Here are presented some examples of expansion activities.

One group spotted as an educational problem their inability to get the most benefit from the Sunday sermon. They developed a program which encouraged parishioners to digest thoughtfully, in personal terms, what had been presented in the sermon. At the Sunday service, the clergyman handed out outlines of his sermon, and after the service all interested persons in the congregation went to the basement. Here they formed discussion groups led by trained participants. Each group discussed the sermon and reported questions and findings 40 minutes later. The clergyman then spent 20 minutes answering the questions in an open forum.

The members of another training group recalled from personal experience that adult instruction classes for new members were conducted through a series of eight lectures to classes numbering 30 to 40 persons. They also remembered that very little audience participation occurred during the "question period" following the lecture -- a situation which they and the clergyman felt should be remedied. In order to improve this educational opportunity and, at the same time, to stimulate more persons later to form training groups, the clergyman and the participants planned and conducted these instruction classes in the following way. First, the clergyman presented a 45-minute lecture. Then the audience formed into small discussion groups of 6 to 8 persons for 20 minutes. Serving as discussion leaders, trained participants helped the groups formulate questions and identify points that needed clarifying. When the whole class reconvened, questions were treated by the clergyman, with open forum participation after each question.

These examples illustrate only two ways in which participants, with the clergyman's cooperation, have helped improve educational activities that were open to the congregation.

It is not always feasible at first to try to improve existing activities, and so other channels of expansion peculiar to the local situation must sometimes be used. Occasionally church organizations provide an alternate way of expanding. Obviously training groups should not tamper with educational activities that are controlled by autonomous organizations or official planning groups without their consent and invitation. Sometimes, however, members of a church organization wish to know more about the developing Plan. In one case, participants of a training group met with various church organizations and helped each of them conduct a colloquy in which they all explored the Indiana Plan and how it could better serve as an educational tool for the whole congregation. These efforts resulted in drawing more persons into training group activities.

Another way in which the trainees can expand the program is through developing needed educational activities as revealed by a congregational survey. The training group can accomplish this by planning and sponsoring series of programs that give parishioners a chance to fill educational needs that they recognize. The informal survey usually reveals several subjects or topics that people feel they need to learn more about. In one case, a series of four educational programs was prompted by parents' need for exploring and finding solutions to the difficulties they encounter while trying to rear their children to be Christians.

Another training group planned and sponsored a series of meetings in which people could explore and try to understand better the recent changes in the rites and services of their church. A brief glimpse of the manner in which these meetings were conducted will illustrate how and why these meetings aroused interest in broadening the Indiana Plan in this church.

In our example-meeting, the significance of "Baptism" was explored. The program began with 15 trained participants discussing for 30 minutes what baptism is, what it means, and what obligations it brings. While they discussed, 25 other interested members of the congregation listened. They were seated informally around three sides of the discussion group and close to it. The frank unrehearsed discussion by the trained participants revealed several problems and misunderstandings that people often avoid because they do not wish to take the risk of appearing ignorant. The audience began to recognize that the training group participants were not lay theologians with special knowledge, but fellow parishioners who, like themselves, needed some new understandings and were searching for them. After 30 minutes, the topic had been opened up and the trained participants pushed back their chairs to merge with the audience into one large face-to-face circle. Then the entire group spent 45 minutes exploring further the meaning of baptism. The clergyman allowed himself to be used sparingly as a subject authority, usually when historical and factual information were relevant to the discussion. He did not try to make a lecture out of each question that was asked.

Now this group of parishioners, made up of trained and untrained persons, did not learn everything there was to know historically and theologically about baptism. But the participants did identify aspects of baptism which bothered them the most -- which they were most ready to learn about. On these points they gained some new insights, and the theology and history they saw a need for was brought to bear. Also, they began to recognize that there were various ways of learning in church groups. After this series of meetings, the way was open for many new parishioners to form interest groups for participation training and for more intensive exploration of needs as they recognized them.

If the Indiana Plan is operating in several churches within a close geographical area, there are two particularly effective ways of illustrating the outward movement or expansion of the program. One way is through interchurch meetings for the participants of training groups from nearby churches of the same communion. These have proved to be highly successful when they begin with a "potluck" dinner followed by an informal program during which people compare their back-home adult education programs and explore common educational problems of program development.

Another type of interchurch educational activity involves participants of nearby churches who meet to participate in an educational program on a religious subject of common interest.

The reader must remember that the few examples of expansion cited here are not to be considered as the only proper ways of expanding the program. They serve only to illustrate specifically a general educational idea: that the program must move outward. It can do so (a) through individuals working separately and (b) through planned educational activities in which individuals participate cooperatively.

What happens to a training group after its initial expansion efforts? Any number of things might happen, depending upon the local situation. For example, it may (and usually should) help organize other training groups; it may continue to plan series of expanded programs for the parish; it may continue to meet periodically as a discussion group to satisfy additional learning needs of the participants.

After other groups have been trained, more and more trained persons will be able to work together meaningfully and purposefully in the congregation. An increasing number of trained persons will be drawn into the joint task of planning and participating in a variety of educational activities that make up the total church family educational endeavor.

D. CONSOLIDATING THE PLAN

As the Plan develops through an expansion phase in a church, steps must be taken to capitalize on the interest that it has aroused in participants and in other persons. Consolidating the Plan means capitalizing on this interest so as to establish more firmly the training activities and the varied educational activities that follow in the church. Experience has shown that four consolidation activities are necessary for the full development of the Plan in any church. These four activities stabilize the developing program, provide for its constant improvement and expansion, and ensure its permanence.

1. Provide Continuing Participation Training for Discussion Teamwork. Normally the early expansion efforts will have aroused the interest of several people in the church. These persons should be encouraged and given an opportunity to get into a training group where they can satisfy some personal educational needs, gain a new understanding of their relationship to the whole congregational family, and develop participation skills and insights that will help them to learn productively and to improve the total adult program in the church. It is well to re-emphasize at this point that the Indiana Plan is not a "group discussion program"; that group discussion is employed first as a convenient participation training medium which people can use to practice the disciplines and skills which produce effective adult learning. Beyond that, group discussion is only one among many educational procedures which people should use appropriately to learn together.

When and how this continuing training for additional people is provided will be determined by factors in the local situation, such as (1) the availability of likely opportunities for starting more training groups (such as subject-interest groups), and (2) the availability of trained persons who can serve as trainers in additional starting groups and help coordinate the program.

The need for additional trainers is usually the more pressing problem. There are two ways of obtaining qualified trainers. First, the trainer who initiated the Plan in the local church can recruit persons he has worked with in the initial starting group or groups and help them personally to serve as trainers for new groups. He must choose these persons carefully and supervise them closely. A second way is to send qualified persons to an institute that is designed to train

trainers. These institutes are described more fully
in Chapter V.

2. <u>Provide</u> <u>Advanced</u> <u>Training</u> <u>for</u> <u>Lay</u> <u>Leaders</u>: <u>the</u> <u>Week-</u>
<u>End</u> <u>Clinic</u>. Another way to fortify the developing
Plan is to provide additional training for lay leaders
or potential leaders -- people whose enthusiasm, insights, and skills have been demonstrated during the
progress of the Plan in the local church. If the Indiana Plan is operating in several churches of the same
communion geographically close together, two or three
trainers can conveniently organize and conduct a clinic
during a weekend two or three times each year in a cen-
tral location. In recent years, there has been considerable emphasis on ecumenicity and another possibility
is to have members of different communions come together
for a clinic. This assumes that each group has participated in the Plan.

The main purpose of these clinics is to identify
and discuss ways of improving and expanding adult programs so that participants, congregations, and commun-
ities can profit further from the skills and insights
that develop through the activities arising out of the
Indiana Plan. Goals, procedures, resources, and special educational problems and needs are explored by
the clinic participants. These are educational clinics
in the medical sense of the word: the "body" being
examined should be the Indiana Plan as it exists in
the churches represented. And it is examined by persons
who have had first-hand experience with the "body."

The most successful clinics have been those attended
by from 15 to 30 persons who represent 3 to 6 different
congregations in which the Plan is operating. People
from churches which are in different stages of development of the Plan can profitably share their unique yet

similar problems of "Starting," "Expanding," and "Con-solidating" -- particularly if they work together and eat together as a team for two days in an away-from-home experience. This type of clinic is not merely a source of educational insights, new skills, and inspiration. It is a concrete illustration of the outward movement which is so vital to this adult educational program and which characterizes an expanding program.

3. **Evaluate** <u>Progress.</u> Evaluation by participants is an important part of the process of adult learning. Actually, evaluating is the act of finding out to what extent a person or group has accomplished what it set out to do. Unless the goals are known in advance, evaluation is impossible. Without periodic evaluation, goals are lost sight of, programs tend to fall into purposeless, unchanging patterns, inappropriate procedures become habitual, and progress is not pointed out and cannot serve as an incentive.

Evaluation is built in as a necessary ingredient of the Indiana Plan because it leads to:
- Increased awareness of goals.
- Increased awareness that something should happen as a result of programs.
- Adjusting of programs to meet needs participants recognize.
- Opportunities for adjusting goals.
- Sharing of results by participants.

In the Starting Phase, evaluation occurs at each session because it is a means by which training groups develop. During expansion it is important as a means of "feeling the pulse" of the developing Plan.

After expansion has begun to broaden the Plan in the church, it is time for all concerned to identify its results in terms of the educational goals of the church. This must be done if the Plan is to be adjusted

103

to the educational needs of an increasing number of
people in the congregation and established as a long-
range program. If the Plan starts, for example, in
the fall and develops beyond the original training
group or groups, an over-all evaluation is usually
necessary six to eight months later (in the spring.)
An effective way of accomplishing this is to have an
evaluation meeting open to all participants and interested persons so that results and deficiencies may be
identified and made known. These findings are needed
as a guide for the planning and establishing of a
productive long-range program. Regular and careful
evaluation is essential to the continued success of
this educational adventure.

4. Establish the Plan as a Long-Range Program. After
    the Plan has expanded beyond the initial training
    group activities and initial expansion efforts have
    been evaluated as a means of accomplishing the educa-
    tional goals of the church, the future task of the
    Plan in that church should be defined. The question
    is, "How can the developing program be better adapted
    to the local needs and problems of this church?" An
    effective answer to this question is a blueprint of
    the way in which the Plan should develop during the
    next few months.

    It is important to establish the Plan with some
    degree of permanence. Thus there is an advantage to
    planning the second year's activities in advance, even
    if details can be only tentatively agreed upon, because
    people can look forward to scheduled events.

    Who should do the long-range planning? Inevitably
    the clergyman and most other persons who have been
    involved in the Plan feel that they have a stake in
    its development, and these feelings should not be

discouraged. And, since by this time several of the
trained persons have acquired skills in program planning, this is an opportunity for them to use those
skills. At least a large committee of trained persons
(and a clergyman) should participate in the long-range
planning of events that are within their jurisdiction.

In churches which have no official Adult Education Committee, the participants or a committee of
them usually begin to operate in an official capacity
when the need for such an organization is recognized.
In instances where such committees already exist, they
have been enlarged to admit more trained persons.
Usually some members of existing official planning
committees have been drawn into the program during
its Starting Phase.

E. A SUMMARY

STARTING PHASE

Tasks

Training in group discussion teamwork
 Leadership
 Group participation
Practicing group discussion teamwork
 Leadership
 Group participation

Purposes

1. To discover common educational needs and explore relevant religious teachings cooperatively in terms of
their significance to participants.

2. To provide a laboratory in which people can develop skills in the following common problem areas of adult religious education: responsible leadership and group participation, communication, goal setting, and evaluation. These skills are needed to equip persons to learn together and to broaden the program in the church.

3. To provide a laboratory in which people can use interpersonal relationships as a resource for better understanding themselves and each other as learners and children of God. The group will develop into a learning team as participants accept each other as unique individuals and face the personal relationships and responsibilities that make teamwork possible.

EXPANDING PHASE

Tasks

• Provide continuing participation training for discussion teamwork

• Provide periodic advanced training for lay leaders

• Evaluate the developing program in terms of the goals of the church

• Establish a long-range educational program

Purposes

1. To provide for continually broadening trained leadership and group participation.

2. To provide means of improving the developing program and readjusting it to the educational needs of the congregation.

3. To stabilize and maintain the developing program.

F. EDUCATIONAL GROUP PROCEDURES USED IN THE INDIANA PLAN

INSTITUTE

In the Indiana Plan the institute is a 5-day series of training sessions designed to equip clergymen and lay educational leaders with the skills and insights necessary for initiating the Indiana Plan and guiding its development in local churches. It is the initial training course for trainers. See Chapter V, Section C, for further information.

CLINIC

In the Indiana Plan, the clinic is a two-day conference (usually held on weekends) conducted periodically in any geographical area in which the Plan is operating in several churches. It is planned and led by trainers; the participants are from 15 to 30 lay leaders who are involved in the plan in local churches. The clinic should be designed primarily to promote the insights and skills necessary for the constant adaptation of the Plan to local educational needs.

GROUP DISCUSSION

In the "Starting" phase of the Indiana Plan, group discussion is adapted as a training tool to develop participant skills and insights necessary for productive group learning. This adaptation of group discussion has been called "participation training."[3] Usually a training group has from 12 to 15 volunteer members who meet with a trainer for 10 to 15 sessions of

---

[3]See _Participation Training for Adult Education_, by Paul Bergevin and John McKinley (Bethany Press, 1965) for a description of participation training as an educational technology.

from 2 to 2 1/2 hours in length. Beyond the "Starting" phase of the Plan, group discussion is only one among many group learning procedures that must be used appropriately in a broad, varied program of activities.

SOME OTHER GROUP PROCEDURES

These basic group procedures[4] and numerous combinations of them are often used in the broad program that develops through the Indiana Plan in local churches:

Speech	Panel	Committee
Interview	Panel-forum	Seminar
Speech-forum	Symposium	Role-playing
Colloquy	Symposium-forum	Forum

---

[4]See _Adult Education Procedures_, by Paul Bergevin, Dwight Morris, and Robert M. Smith (New York: Seabury Press, 1963), for a description of various group procedures.

CHAPTER IV

EDUCATIONAL RESULTS OF THE INDIANA PLAN

A. INTRODUCTION

A learning program in the church should help participants accomplish specific tasks and show increasing progress in several
areas which results in better understanding and fellowship.
Specific observable results of an effective program based on
the Indiana Plan are described in this chapter. Section B
describes and explains areas of personal growth and definite
criteria by which growth can be identified. Section C describes
results in terms of changes in parish life as perceived by
local church practitioners across the country. Desirable changes
in personal growth and in parish life and practices are highly
related outcomes; both are presented, however, in the interest
of describing the results from more than one viewpoint.

B. AREAS AND CRITERIA OF PERSONAL GROWTH

What are some of the areas in which personal growth of participants can be observed?
    1. Creative self-expression
    2. Acceptance of personal responsibility
    3. Cooperation in a common task
    4. Better communication
    5. Self-examination
    6. Self-guidance
    7. Sensitivity to individual needs

How do we know when we are reaching these results? What
are some of the criteria which help to determine some degree
of achievement reached? In the following examination of each
of these areas of desirable results several points are listed
which can be used as guide posts or a checklist to determine
to a degree the maturity and progress achieved.

1. Creative Self-expression. Creative self-expression is
mainly a result of freedom of expression. When we believe that

109

we will be understood and respected we can pour out our ideas and opinions more freely. Such freedom of expression may not be creative in the sense that something new is created for the first time. It can, however, result in persons fashioning ideas and situations which are new, original, and thus creative so far as those persons are concerned.

Creative self-expression can develop as a result of training and experience in informal adult education. It is not just a pouring-out process, which can very well be quite uncreative. Freedom of expression encourages the first stage of pouring out, of learning to loosen up so that we feel unafraid to use our talents. Creative self-expression is the second stage of learning to communicate verbally. It is a stage in which we learn how to make organized use of freedom of expression; where we construct our often loosely organized -- and sometimes carelessly considered -- thoughts into a more disciplined framework of self-expression.

Freedom unrestrained is really not freedom but often results in anarchy; therefore, it is vital that participants discipline themselves and each other in this learning procedure. They learn to accept responsibility for what they say and do. Scholarly interpretation is a necessary and valuable resource in any learning adventure, but there must be also freedom for us to deal with these interpretations in such a way that we can make them meaningful to us. We don't limit our activity to a recitation of the ideas of others. We bring ourselves into an understanding relationship with other persons and ideas. If we are to act, and to give, we've got to understand how and why and where.

As this Plan evolves successfully we will observe certain characteristics of creative self-expression:

a. A participant expresses what is for him a new, unusual, or unexpected idea or way of dealing with a problem.

b. Group participants and leaders help to bring an idea, which might be new to the one expressing it, into full view.

c. Learners become more willing to seek out and use various resource materials and persons. They are also willing to help develop some of their own materials.

d. Learners express their feelings and ideas without fear and learn to accept the expressions of fellow learners.

e. More volunteers offer their help and recommendations on policy and procedures in the educational program.

f. A participant will offer an idea which he admittedly knows he personally cannot develop. He offers the nebulous idea without fear of others labelling it as crude or unpolished.

2. Acceptance of Personal Responsibility. The success of this learning program depends on all of the persons involved. Subject matter becomes meaningful to the participants because they eventually bring the resource material (it may be a picture, a book, a speech) into relationship with some other experiences they have had or are having. To do this is the personal responsibility of each participant. Acceptance of this responsibility is a prerequisite of personal development and growth within the learning group. A learner in this Plan cannot gain its full value if he sits back and listens only, allowing others to take full responsibility. When we accept personal responsibility for the educational program, we become involved in a living situation in which learning takes place through our efforts.

How can we tell when we are assuming our share of the job? A number of actions point clearly toward growth and maturity through acceptance of responsibility:

a. The participant does what he says he will do. If he volunteers to act as leader for the next meeting he makes preparation and carries out the task.

b. Participants read their assigned resource materials and come prepared to use time efficiently.

c. Participants learn and practice the rules of the learning procedure used.

d. A learner who actively participates in the following ways is accepting responsibility:
- saying what he knows or believes
- listening carefully when others talk

111

- helping others to clarify their thoughts
- suggesting new ways of carrying on
- helping the leader when he's in trouble
- recognizing the need for, and suggesting, such activities as evaluating and summarizing
- helping to arrange physical properties (such as tables and chairs) for meetings
- helping persons to stay on the subject

e. Participants volunteer for committee work and for the various chores necessary in this kind of learning activity.

f. Participants plan their other activities so that they can regularly attend the learning program on time.

g. Participants freely offer suggestions for improvement which they know may cause them more work.

3. <u>Cooperation</u> <u>in</u> <u>a</u> <u>Common</u> <u>Task</u>. Learning to work together toward common ends is basic to the Indiana Plan for Adult Religious Education. Cooperation, or working together, in this Plan is based on the idea that each person should take on his share of the job.

We begin to recognize how to make the most of our talents in a cooperative enterprise when we learn to listen to others' views and analyze and select them in terms of the mutual good. For example, we learn to stand our ground for a point when it seems necessary to us. But we do it because we believe it worthwhile for the learning team as well as for us.

Some criteria which help us determine the progress we make in learning to work together are as follows:

a. <u>We</u> <u>learn</u> <u>to</u> <u>think</u> <u>of</u> <u>others</u>. We learn to give more of ourselves to those with whom we are learning without seeking a direct or immediate reward. When a learner begins actively and enthusiastically to listen to others and to assist in the development of others' points of view, it is clear that he is growing. Rather than push his ideas over so that he can feel the prideful satisfaction of winning over some opposition, he learns to explain his ideas because they seem to him to be of value to those with whom he is working. Thinking of our learning problems and expressing them from a group point of view, as well as an individual one, is a clear sign that we are bursting out of the confines of self.

b. **We become less interested in who gets the credit.** Another sign of growth toward maturity is shown when we become noticeably less concerned about who gets the credit. We no longer withdraw and sulk or growl privately to others when we feel that we have been slighted. When we do not have to be in the limelight to be productive we are beginning to dedicate ourselves as co-workers. A sign of immaturity is revealed when "we must be the whole show or we won't play." Other persons who we think may not be "fast thinkers" or "smart" are needed as much as we, and they need to know they are needed.

c. **We both tell and ask.** Growth in ability to ask relevant questions and thoughtfully consider the answers is a criterion of progress in this learning plan. Well-chosen questions which reflect our desire to know what others think, and why, are as important to the learning process as meaningful declarations. When we can observe our fellow learners beginning to establish a balance between telling and asking, growth is taking place.

d. **We keep on topic and goal.** Most topics have a way of reminding us of ideas which may have little or no relevance to our stated goal. The danger here is that a few participants may start to talk about irrelevant subjects, drawing others off the track and completely ignoring the previously agreed upon topic and goal. As time goes on we should see specific evidence of self-discipline in the group as shown by a firmer will to stick to the topic and by frequent reference to the established goals. When this is apparent, the group is maturing.

e. **We control our emotions.** Every well-conducted learning program will develop situations of conflict and misunderstanding. This is normal in a dynamic situation. It is not pleasant to have someone disagree with an opinion which we have kept in our opinion-vault for many years. We have a large emotional investment in some of our own opinions, and it is perfectly natural to resist any threat to their security. We feel quite uncomfortable when someone challenges it unless we know how to work and learn together. Our first reaction is to become angry or upset. However, if we are improving our relationships with our fellow-learners and learning more about ourselves, we often come to understand the necessity for revising our opinions and behavior -- and we do so with much less emotional tension than would have been thought possible at the beginning of the learning adventure.

f. **We do not insist on agreement.** We desire the approval of others. We want them to agree with us. When they do we feel more secure -- our ego is sustained. Such a desire is beneficial to our well being in some ways and harmful in others; harmful when we use it to feel more important and prideful with less concern about how our fellow-learners on the team are coming along; beneficial because it is healthy for us to feel that we belong and are wanted by others. Now the desire for self-protection and support is a perfectly healthy desire for acceptance. But the others on the learning team have feelings of security as vital as ours. It is important, therefore, for us to be as seriously concerned for them as for ourselves. We are less anxious to expect complete agreement when we (1) know the reasons for disagreement, (2) begin to recognize that others have a right to, and a need for, a personal point of view, and (3) realize that honest difference of opinion often assists in the learning process. It can help us present our position more carefully and examine it more critically.

We are advancing toward maturity through learning together and we begin to identify agreement and disagreement for what they are -- parts of the learning process, instead of opportunities to prove someone right and someone wrong.

But it is not wholly sufficient to recognize the value of differences of opinion. Sometimes it is necessary to reconcile these differences in order to move forward in the educational program. The degree of reconciliation accomplished by persons

with different views is an important indication of the extent
of maturity achieved.

     g. <u>Decisions</u> <u>by</u> <u>consensus</u> <u>form</u> <u>a</u> <u>core</u> <u>for</u> <u>operations</u>.
Consensus as used here can result in coming to a workable solu-
tion to a problem, usually tentative, by sort of an amalgam of
the several points of view expressed. Consensus is arrived at
by compromise.

     Cooperation in a common task is necessary if a group is
to accomplish anything. It is a major step toward growth and
maturity. Teamwork does not usually develop because of an
eloquent speech on cooperation. It comes about by experiencing
cooperative endeavors in actual situations in which we become
increasingly aware of the need for cooperation.

     It should be understood, however, that learning groups do
not make group decisions -- except when they are determining
educational goals, tasks, resources, and procedures. Members
of learning groups usually help one another to understand their
mutual learning problems. They do not "decide" for each other
concerning solutions to individual learning problems. It is
each learner's job to try to understand how other persons and
religious teachings can help him. Participants do not make
majority decisions to validate or invalidate religious teachings.

     When we express opinions we make a contribution toward
the development of the learning group. Our idea may be an
expression which fits into the majority opinion. If so, our
task is not difficult. If, however, we disagree with the majority to the extent that we find it difficult to work with them,
we have a decision to make which is not always easy. If there
is too much uniqueness, we can't get enough agreement to do
anything together. If there is too much emphasis on complete
agreement the potential force of the individual as a unique
contributor is lost. We must reach a balance, therefore, between destructive competition and submission to a group will.

There are mature ways of dealing with the problem of our disagreement with majority opinion. We may accept majority opinion with reservations and still try to convince others -- by open, honest and legitimate means -- that some modification of their views might be necessary. Or we may be unwilling to accept the basic views of the majority and thus become an active minority. Difference of opinion in either case is not in itself an indication of immaturity. Minority ideas are vital factors in the progress of the group. When both the minority and the majority use mature ways to discover a common ground for moving ahead concerted action often results.

h. <u>Trivial</u> <u>matters</u> <u>are</u> <u>put</u> <u>in</u> <u>their</u> <u>place</u>. Another encouraging indication of growth is that we become increasingly able to attack the work to be done and the problems to be solved. As we mature as a learning team, we see more emphasis placed on accomplishing the learning task than on efforts to subdue those who are perceived as obstructionists.

4. <u>Better</u> <u>Communication</u>. In this Plan communication is used to denote the sharing of thoughts and feelings. In every stage of development in this learning procedure, emphasis is placed on saying what we mean as well as we can and on listening. We try to transmit our thoughts and ideas in a simple, straight-forward, well-organized manner. We also try to understand what others are trying to say to us. Talking does not necessarily mean there is communication. When we say something which others can understand and when they listen to and understand what we say, we are communicating with them.

Indications of our concern for better communication are noted:

a. when we organize our ideas on the subject in what seems to us to be a logical fashion. This might be done in outline form on paper before we attend the meeting.

b. when we avoid the use of indefinite references and comparisons. "I read somewhere or maybe somebody told me . . ." or "they always say that . . ."

c. when we learn to be specific. We use illustrations and describe situations which mean something to those with whom we are learning.

d. when we listen to and think about others' contributions before we try to answer. Failure here is one of the most serious blocks to effective communication. We may have a pet idea which we will not have challenged. When someone disagrees with it, we don't listen honestly to what he says. We only wait for him to stop talking so that we can tell him the "truth." And sometimes we don't even wait for him to stop talking but interrupt him thereby causing friction which undermines the progress made.

e. when we ask for clarification or amplification of contributions made.

f. when we have less misunderstanding among participants regarding assignments, commitments, and educational goals.

g. when we listen carefully to others, so as to learn how they organize and express their points of view.

We become aware of the need for clear, concise, well-organized expression and we try to practice it constantly -- yet without such concern with its mechanics that we become fearful of saying the wrong thing or the right one in a disorganized way. We realize that most of the members of the learning team are in the same situation, and we do the best we can.

5. <u>Self-examination</u>. Together learners employ group self-examination in this Plan during evaluation or critique sessions. Further achievements can be realized through private self-examination. It is helpful to take an occasional personal inventory of how we handle problems and work with others, and whether our reactions and attitudes are in keeping with the basic goal of adult religious education. To be sure, we don't always see ourselves as clearly as we should. We are often hindered by prejudice, sentimentalism, and pride. But we can learn to be more objective if we examine some of the things we have thought and said and done as they relate to our effort to grow into more mature persons.

When a reasonable degree of self-examination takes place, it can help improve our ability to learn and work with others.

The wrong kind of self-examination can act as a corrosive element preventing the very thing we seek. We should try to maintain a balance by looking honestly at what has happened, by being pleased with what seems to be satisfactory, and trying sincerely to improve those areas where we slipped.

Evidence, in terms of behavior, of the value of proper self-examination shows up in learning situations. Sometimes these changed behavior patterns may result from sources other than self-examination. But it will be observed that in those groups where self-examination is employed as a learning device over a period of eight to ten meetings, behaviors listed below tend to be more evident than in those groups in which it was not used.

    a. We reveal a heightened consciousness of our behavior by the kind of program topics and goals we suggest.

    b. We make more comments like these: "I didn't realize before. . . ." "I see now that I am. . . ." "I could be wrong."

    c. We ask the other participants' opinions about what we say, do, and think.

    d. We become more willing to admit breaches in group teamwork.

    e. We listen more attentively.

    f. We hesitate less to ask others on the learning team for help.

    g. We display a less defensive attitude.

    h. We can discuss our own area of interest and our pet ideas with an increasing degree of objectivity.

Caution should be exercised to see that the self-examination reveals points which will help us to become a better participant and not become an occasion for maudlin behavior.

6. _Self-guidance_. Self-guidance is a kind of personal direction we exert on ourselves when we learn how to discipline and control ourselves. It is a prime factor in our growth as Christians. Guiding ourselves does not mean that we separate ourselves from God or from the corporate fellowship as super-individualists, but rather that we give greater service by helping our fellow

learners and ourselves as we learn how to direct and use our talents. As self-guidance increases the need for external control diminishes.

In the last analysis we learn as individuals. Nobody else can learn for us. We must not, therefore, neglect those skills which help us to accept personal responsibility to think and do for ourselves. As we learn to handle our own problems better, we are also able to make a more helpful contribution to the development of maturity in people.

We can handle subject matter (content) more intelligently when we accept responsibility to communicate effectively, and to cooperate in a common task (process). So our learning problem is not process-centered or content-centered -- but both. During the learning activity we emphasize what we are learning -- ideas and facts (content) and also the skills and actions which make the subject matter meaningful and useful (process).

The degree to which we have achieved constructive self-guidance is often revealed by the way we behave in learning situations. The following points are criteria by which we can evaluate, to some degree, our progress in this area of development:

a. We rely less and less on the nominal leaders[1] and accept an increasing amount of responsibility for all phases of the learning experience.

b. We volunteer rather than wait to be asked.

c. We personally follow up the learning experiences and apply new understandings.

d. We do a more thorough job of the assignments we have volunteered to accept.

e. We take a more active part in relating the topic and the verbal expressions and resource materials supporting the topic.

7. Sensitivity to Individual Needs. It is generally accepted that a large part of our service to God is realized through

---

[1] The role of the "leader" is treated in detail in Participation Training for Adult Education (Bethany Press, 1965), by the present authors.

other persons. Precisely how we can improve in our understanding of, and relationships with, others probably varies somewhat with each person. We do know that we must associate with each other. And by this association we can learn something about and from each other. We know, further, that by practicing certain skills we can improve our understanding of ourselves in relation to others. Such skills as communicating better with others and accepting responsibility with others and for others' welfare contribute to individual and corporate growth.

As the learning teams mature, evidence that we are developing sensitivity to others' needs is revealed in how we behave with and toward our fellow learners. This is one reason why we need to examine our progress together in this area periodically. and systematically during regular learning situations. We will not get at satisfactory information by having participants fill out questionnaires on these points. Factors in the actual experience must be openly discussed and evaluated. There are certain questions which we can use as a measuring stick to assess growth in sensitivity to others:

a. Are we learning to accept others as fellow human beings with regard to their: (1) physical appearance; (2) race; (3) religion; (4) social position; (5) level of schooling; (6) habits; (7) sex; (8) contributions to the learning team; (9) opinions?

b. Do we refer to the contributions of others?

c. Do we help others, who may have joined the learning team late, to become acclimated?

d. Do we suggest or accept resources appropriate to all group members in terms of their reading ability, hearing ability, endurance, etc.?

e. Can we accept people as they are without labelling them right or wrong, good or bad?

f. Do we value the person as much or more than the idea?

g. Do we make people feel that their contributions are worthy: (1) by listening carefully; (2) by trying to help those who find difficulty in expressing themselves; (3) by being cheerful and pleasant?

h. Are we willing to help others without blaming them?

i. Can we keep our points of disagreement on a friendly, objective basis?

j. Do we try to keep minority views before the group?

k. Are we moving away from the reward and punishment philosophy and beginning to do things because they need to be done without too much concern with credit or failure?

C. RESULTS REPORTED BY FIELD PRACTITIONERS

This section summarizes perceived results of using the Indiana Plan in local churches. It is based on the reports of ten selected local church trainers from different denominations who were known to be highly-skilled practitioners. Their experience ranged from one to 9 years of programming with Indiana Plan applications in local churches. In addition, most of them were certified institute staff trainers and qualified observers. The results reported here are, therefore, the kinds of results one might expect when the Indiana Plan is operating with skilled direction.

The results are reported in terms of frequency of trainer-perceived changes (1) in individuals, (2) in adult education programs in the church, (3) in formal church organizations, (4) in congregational spirit, (5) in worship services, (6) in the relation of the congregation to other congregations, (7) in congregational decision making, (8) in community outreach, (9) in the way the clergyman is perceived by the parishioners, and (10) in other areas.

1. Kinds of Perceived Changes in Individual Participants. The data from the 10 trained observers indicated perceived changes in seven different areas of behavior. Obviously in some cases the same kind of change is described by two or more criteria.

a. More effective personal relationships:

    1. with self ------------------------- high frequency of positive change[2]
    2. with spouse ----------------------- high frequency of positive change
    3. with other parishioners ------------ high frequency of positive change
    4. with fellow employees ------------- medium frequency of positive change
    5. with God ------------------------- medium frequency of positive change

These changes are attributed to increased understandings and new attitudes developed mainly through participation training. Data supporting items #4 and #5 were not readily identifiable or verifiable and were in most cases qualified by question marks and terms such as "likely."

b. Increased willingness to work:

    1. in a teaching or leadership role ---- high frequency of positive change
    2. in a service role (including
       committee, boards, commissions) ---- high frequency of positive change[3]
    3. in community activities ---------- medium frequency of positive change
    4. in inter-denominational activities --- low frequency of positive change

c. Improved stewardship:

    1. of money ------------------------- low frequency of positive change
    2. of time given to church ------------ high frequency of positive change
    3. of talent given to church ---------- high frequency of positive change

d. Increased willingness and ability to
recruit new church members ----------- medium frequency of positive change

e. Increased willingness[4] to study primary
materials of religious education (the Bible,
pamphlets, study materials, etc.) ----- medium frequency of positive change

f. Increased ability to understand written
materials ------------------------------ low frequency of positive change

g. Increased willingness to help other programs
in the church to deal with problems of day-
to-day living ------------------------ medium frequency of positive change

2. Kinds of Perceived Changes in the Adult Programs of the Church

  a. Increased number of persons attending - medium frequency of positive change

  b. More active participation -------------- high frequency of positive change

  c. Better use of evaluation procedures --- medium frequency of positive change

  d. More realistic, effective goals --------- high frequency of positive change

  e. More effective planning of programs ----- high frequency of positive change

---

[2]High frequency indicates changes in 70 percent, or more, of the reported cases; medium frequency was 30 to 70 percent; low frequency was below 30 percent.

[3]Objective data were reported to be not usually available or verifiable.

[4]These changes were only for persons involved in the training program.

f. More effective leaders ------------------ high frequency of positive change

g. More persons involved in planning ------ high frequency of positive change

h. More appropriate group learning
   procedures used ------------------------ high frequency of positive change

i. Improvement of Sunday morning adult
   programs ------------------------------- high frequency of positive change

j. More small-group educational programs
   to meet a variety of needs ------------- high frequency of positive change

k. More large-group educational programs
   to meet a variety of needs ----------- medium frequency of positive change

l. Improved teacher training programs ----- high frequency of positive change

3. Kinds of Perceived Changes Within the Formal Organizations in the Church

   a. Educational programs to train organizational
      leaders in their duties ---------------- low frequency of positive change

   b. More effective committee work -------- medium frequency of positive change

   c. Clarification of goals ------------------ high frequency of positive change

   d. Clarification of tasks --------------- medium frequency of positive change

4. Kinds of Perceived Changes in the Congregational Spirit

   a. Increased accepting-helping-sharing
      relationships ------------------------- high frequency of positive change

   b. Increased willingness to work to-
      gether ------------------------------ medium frequency of positive change

Also reported in 1/3 of the responses in this category were reactions described
as overt tension and jealousy exhibited by persons in the congregation who were not
in the training programs. Some of these feelings appear to be natural in the early
phase of program development.

5. Kinds of Perceived Changes in the Worship Program

Many individualized responses indicated a medium frequency of positive changes
that could best be summarized as:

   - increased regularity of attendance
   - more adult participation in the services
   - willingness and desire to experiment with different worship formats to meet
     the needs of persons in different age groups and with different orientations
     to worship.

6. Kinds of Perceived Changes in the Relation of the Congregation to Other Congregations

   a. Increased fellowship with other
      congregations ------------------------- high frequency of positive change

   b. Increased cooperation with other
      congregations ------------------------ medium frequency of positive change

7. Kinds of Perceived Changes in the Way Decisions are Made that Affect the Entire Congregation

Positive changes were reported with medium frequency, and these were individualized responses, such as:

- "less dependence on minister"
- "increased willingness to express differences"
- "governing body no longer a rubber stamp; they now openly identify attempts at manipulation"
- "more views are brought out into the open"
- "some not in the training program are less cooperative"

8. Kinds of Perceived Changes in the Community Outreach of the Congregation

   a. Improved outreach through individuals ------------------------- medium frequency of positive change

   b. Improved outreach through organized activities --------------------------- low frequency of positive change

9. Kinds of Perceived Changes in the Way the Clergyman is Perceived by the Parishioners

   a. Clergyman's educational role is more functional ------------------------- medium frequency of positive change

   b. Parishioners' idea of the clergyman's role has changed so that he now has more time to use his individual resources more effectively -------------------- medium frequency of positive change

10. Other Results

These results were identified mainly in personal terms by trainers, most of whom were clergymen:

- I feel less guilt when things don't get done by the laity
- I'm more tolerant of imperfection
- Clarification of personal goals
- I work better with groups
- More questions get raised
- Better use of resources in the Church
- Improved youth program
- Large leadership potential moved from apathy to involvement
- Changes in churches tend to take place in spurts or peaks of activity

124

CHAPTER V

NEW PERSPECTIVES ON THE INDIANA PLAN

A. INTRODUCTION

This chapter is an attempt to identify aspects and challenges
related to the Indiana Plan that have come into prominence
during the 12 years since the program was inaugurated in the
book Design for Adult Education in the Church. Section B describes three major forces now affecting the church as an educational institution. An effort is made to show how the Indiana
Plan can help meet the challenges in each of these areas.

Section C (following) describes briefly the printed materials and training programs now available to local church practitioners. A summary of research findings directly related to
the Indiana Plan is also presented. Section D enumerates and
briefly describes some major pitfalls of local church application that have been identified in field practice.

B. THE SETTING: THE PRESENT STATE OF THE CHURCH[1]

In the decade since Design for Adult Education in the Church
was published, the institutional church has been undergoing
changes that present new opportunities and challenges to its
adult membership. The authors wish to identify three develop-
ments which seem likely to have lasting effects on the church,
its structure and its mission, and to suggest some implications
these trends have in relation to the pattern for adult religious
education set forth throughout the book.

1. Ecumenical Progress. A major trend through Christendom is
evidenced in the area of increased interchurch relationships.
Conversations and negotiations within denominations and between

---
[1]Section B was written by the Rev. Roye M. Frye.

them are accelerating at a rapid pace.[2] The spirit of ecumenicity is making inroads into historical boundaries that have separated churches for centuries. This phenomenon is prevalent not only between Protestant churches, but includes, as well, the Roman Catholic and Orthodox sectors of Christendom. Less extensive or dramatic, but of increasing significance, are mounting interfaith efforts between Christians and Jews to engage in dialogue and cooperative ventures aimed at community betterment and mutual understanding. This major trend is still largely characterized by conversations and ecclesiastical levels "higher" than the local church. "Grass roots" efforts to participate in the movement are not as evident.

> The Indiana Plan can be used to enhance interchurch and interfaith engagement in the exchange of ideas and understandings needed to promote greater unity at the local level. For example, this could be accomplished by enlisting participants from different denominations to be trained in Group Discussion teamwork.[3] Following this phase of their training, participants could be encouraged to sponsor interchurch or interfaith meetings involving more members of their respective congregations.[4]

2. Involvement in Public Affairs. Increasing efforts are being made by churches to help remedy major social ills of our day such as war, racism and poverty. Due to the contrasting images church members have of the role of the institutional

---

[2] For a summary of current union negotiations in America, see the extensive listing in the 1969 Yearbook of American Churches, Laurie B. Whitman (3d.), National Council of Churches, New York, NY, pp. 201-205.

[3] See Chapter II, Section A.

[4] See "Expansion Phase" in Chapter III and Section G, Chapter II.

church, its involvement in socio-political problems is evoking widespread conflicts at every level of its membership.[5]

While attitudes vary widely regarding the church's appropriate stance in this area, they tend to gravitate toward one of two poles. The first, which emphasizes the church's pastoral ministry, focuses on the individual. His nurture is seen as the paramount and perhaps sole concern of the church's efforts. This position assumes that an adequate ministry to the individual member will enable him to function effectively as a Christian in every sphere of his life including the contributions he can make to the solution of society's ills. Those who espouse this view tend to denigrate corporate efforts by the church to alleviate or solve such problems on the grounds that they violate the time-honored American doctrine of the separation of church and state.

The second view is strongly influenced by the prophetic element in the church's heritage. Proponents of this view contend that the urgency and scope of contemporary social problems demand a more concerted and powerful approach by the church than can be achieved through individuals acting separately. Those who hold this view insist that the church's ministry to our society will be almost wholly ineffective and irrelevant unless there is corporate commitment to an aggressive program of social action.

Articulate advocates of each position probably represent a minority of church members, albeit a vocal one on each side. The majority between the two extremes express varying degrees of concern and apathy, understanding and confusion. The more the church becomes involved in social issues the greater seems the likelihood of its membership dividing itself increasingly

---

[5]See *To Comfort and To Challenge: A dilemma of the contemporary church*, Charles Y. Glock, Benjamin B. Ringer and Earl R. Babbie, U. of California Press, Berkeley, California, 1967.

between one pole or the other. The undecided or frustrated may leave the field of battle altogether.

Whatever decision is reached as to what the "political" role of the church will be, commitment of its membership to that decision will be essential to enable the church to carry out a ministry of reconciliation. Presently, the church seems unable to produce a decision that represents a consensus among its membership. Conflicts continue unabated; disunity could result in schism which would render the church impotent as a reconciling agency in society.[6]

The situation is ironic. While ecumenical progress is engendering greater unity between churches, there is a simultaneous increase of disunity within them as they struggle to find an appropriate stance that relates them to the society whose ills they would help alleviate.

While the Indiana Plan can offer no panacea to solve the difficulties inherent in this problem, it can be of help because it offers an approach to learning that enables people to express themselves freely in an atmosphere of mutual acceptance. When the learning climate is cooperative rather than competitive, and the goal is understanding rather than winning, diversity and conflict can be handled without producing schism. Therefore, controversy can lead to understanding, opposing views can be maintained in a creative tension, and the fabric of the church's unity and effectiveness held intact.[7]

3. Intellectual and Emotional Ferment. Historically the church has sought to make its message credible and relevant by

---

[6]"In a span of just eleven years the proportion of American adults who believe that religion is 'losing its influence on American life' has jumped from 14 percent to 67 percent. This, according to George Gallup whose periodic polls yielded this finding, 'represents one of the most dramatic shifts in surveys of American life'" Whitman, Op. Cit., p. 205.

[7]See Chapter II, especially Section E.

casting its doctrines and ethical precepts into the language and thought-forms of each successive age.[8] Emerging today from a pre-scientific worldview, the church is now confronted with the task of translating its faith and ethical system into a form commensurate with the modern scientific mentality.

The age in which we live has spawned an industrial, technological revolution accompanied by urbanization and growing secularism. Modern man tends more and more to take an empirical, scientific approach to reality. How can the church speak to him? In earlier decades of this century, the monumental task of translating its message into contemporary thought-forms seemed virtually impossible. Science and religion appeared to be in direct conflict. However, in recent years, efforts have been made to harmonize these two world views. Inevitably, as in the past, traditional doctrines are undergoing reconstruction.[9]

Intellectually, the church is in a period of transition. This process is fraught with difficulties. The church, as other institutions, does not change quickly. It is protective of tradition. It rightly seeks to safeguard its inheritance and is reluctant to relinquish former modes of expressing its faith. Credibility and relevance, necessary as they are, are not to be achieved by sacrificing the authenticity of its beliefs.

While this situation does not seem to pose the same polarization problem as that of the church's "political" role, it is critical nevertheless. Thousands of Christians rely on the security of time-honored formularies. Other thousands, outside of or on the fringe of the church, by-pass its faith precisely

---

[8] For example, the Greek language and Greek philosophy were utilized in the writing of the New Testament and, later, in formulating the Nicene Creed.

[9] See _Honest to God_ by J.A.T. Robinson, Philadelphia: Westminister Press, 1963; _The Secular City_ by Harvey Cox, New York: The Macmillan Co., 1965; _A Time for Christian Candor_ by James A. Pike, New York: Harper and Row, 1964, and _If This be Heresy_ by James A. Pike, New York: Harper and Row, 1967.

because ancient doctrinal formulations seem not to be understandable or tenable in this contemporary, scientific world.[10]

A major issue is, "How can the church communicate and commend its faith in contemporary terms without disenfranchising an established **majority** whose **allegiance** seems inextricably bound to the hallowed past?"

The complexity, rapidity and scope of changes that are now becoming evident throughout the entire fabric of society is imparting an emotional as well as intellectual impact on the church.

The widening generation gap, the emerging drug culture and quest for transcendent experience, the "New Left," and the depersonalization of life are a sample of the forces compelling the church to reassess its traditional conceptions of its authority, structure and mission.[11]

Long-accepted channels of ecclesiastical authority, the respective roles of clergy and laity, and the functionality of the local church are under relentless scrutiny. A consequent thrust in the direction of innovation and experimentation is apparent particularly in the areas of worship and in new forms of ministry to the community.

The transitional process is proving to be traumatic. Anxiety, confusion and resistance are mixed with hope, courage and joy as this venerable institution seeks to accomplish the necessary restructuring and renewal to be a more effective instrument for meeting contemporary man's religious needs.

---

[10]Defection from the institutional church is particularly high in the 21-29 year age group. See Whitman, Op. Cit., p. 206.

[11]See The Grass Roots Church: A Manifesto for Protestant Renewal by Stephen C. Rose, New York: The Abingdon Press, 1966; and From Tradition to Mission by Wallace E. Fisher, New York: Abingdon Press, 1965.

When an institution is in a period of transition and its membership undergoes the numerous tensions associated with moving from old to new patterns, a prime need is to have maximum responsible participation in the change process.

The challenge here is for the church to engage as many adults as possible in the kind of study that is focused both on the rich heritage of its past and on the intellectual currents of the contemporary scene. An increase of knowledge in both areas is important.

The Indiana Plan can assist in this exploration since in all its phases participants learn how to develop the subject matter of their meetings through the effective use of educational resources.

In addition, the Indiana Plan provides training in responsible participation for everyone, designated leaders and group participants alike. It emphasizes the desirability of establishing goals that are mutually agreed-upon, realistic and attainable. It provides means for continuous appraisal of how people work together and how well they achieve their goals.

We believe this pattern for the religious education of adults can contribute to the continuing process of renewal within the church.

C. NEW TOOLS

During the past 12 years the resources available to practitioners who wish to learn how to apply the Indiana Plan have multiplied. The purpose of this section is to identify the nature and sources of a few of these tools. They are described here under three headings: (1) printed materials that are useful in local church training programs, (2) institute training programs for practitioners, and (3) research findings directly related to Indiana Plan programming.

1. <u>Printed</u> <u>Materials</u>. The small book <u>Participation</u> <u>Training</u> <u>for</u> <u>Adult</u> <u>Education</u> (Bethany Press, 1965) has become a primary training tool for trainers as well as for all other participants in the Starting Phase of the Indiana Plan. It describes the nature of participation training, how it differs from other types of study-discussion groups, common problems of participants, group roles and responsibilities, structural elements of group discussion, procedures for trainers, and the phases of group development. This book is considerably more detailed in its descriptions of the training aspects of the Starting Phase than analogous materials originally described in the book <u>Design</u> <u>for</u> <u>Adult</u> <u>Education</u> <u>in</u> <u>the</u> <u>Church</u> in 1958.

For participants in the Expanding Phase of local church programming, two printed resources are now being used that were not available when the Indiana Plan was first described in book form. <u>Adult</u> <u>Education</u> <u>Procedures</u> (Seabury Press, 1963) by Paul Bergevin, Robert Smith, and Dwight Morris, fully describes 20 group procedures that are tested patterns for effective participation of adults in educational activities. Detailed descriptions make this how-to-do-it manual an indispensable resource for persons who are learning how to plan and conduct educational activities for adults. Several copies of this book are needed when the training group begins planning expanded educational programs of various kinds. Another useful tool for groups engaged in learning how to plan programs is <u>A</u> <u>Guide</u> <u>to</u> <u>Program</u> <u>Planning</u> (Seabury Press, 1963), by John McKinley and Robert Smith. It is useful for each member of the training group to have a copy of this booklet, which describes the nature and procedures of program planning, along with pitfalls to avoid.

2. <u>Institute</u> <u>Training</u> <u>Programs</u> <u>for</u> <u>Practitioners</u>. Practitioners who wish to learn how to use the Indiana Plan in a local church setting normally attend an Indiana Plan institute for Trainers. Fifteen to thirty participants attend an institute. These training programs, usually 5 days in length, are directed by 2 to 5 qualified persons who (a) have been participants in

an institute, (b) have had experience in applying the Indiana Plan and (c) have had additional experience in training trainers. Those qualified persons from Indiana University have been awarded a certificate which certifies that they are "staff trainers." At the present time about 150 persons have been certified. Their names and addresses are available at the Bureau of Studies in Adult Education, Indiana University, for those who wish to inquire about their availability for conducting institutes in various places in this country.

From 5 to 7 of these institutes are conducted each year by the Bureau of Studies in Adult Education on the campus of Indiana University. These institutes are open to all persons who apply, but only 30 persons are accepted for any one institute. Additional institutes are conducted each year by certified persons at other locations in the United States. Most of the latter institutes are sponsored by jurisdictional units of church denominations (such as synods, conferences, and dioceses). Several are co-sponsored by cooperating denominations.

3. Research Findings Related to the Indiana Plan. This section summarizes pertinent findings of formal research studies conducted during the last 10 years that have been directly related to Indiana Plan programming. Most of these studies have been concerned with some aspect of participation training and its applications, partly because this tool lends itself to experimental application and control and partly because there is much to learn about the application and effects of this training procedure. The findings listed here are summarized and include some related conclusions and recommendations that seem to be pertinent to practitioners in churches. The sources[12] referred to in the footnotes are listed in the bibiliography of writings related to the Indiana Plan, which is part of this present volume:

_____

[12]Results of related studies conducted with mental patients are not included in the summary of findings, but these studies are listed in the bibliography.

- Participation Training is a potentially useful tool to increase the understanding and communication between parents and their youth of high school age.[13]

- When youth of high school age and their parents were both engaged in effective participation training group activities there was a significant[14] positive change toward an accepting and supportive atmosphere in the participants' conversations in the home.

- In a 12-session participation training program, training groups that meet once a week are less likely to produce successful training results than groups which (a) meet 2 sessions per week for 6 weeks or (b) hold the first 6 sessions in a week-end retreat setting away from home and the last 6 sessions weekly thereafter.[15]

- In participation training groups which are composed of parents and their high school age children, the participants tend to undergo a large amount of interpersonal stress during training sessions. One obstruction to progress is the parents' unwillingness to acknowledge their need to improve communication in the family. One source of this problem seemed to be the parental need to be in authority as the giver of knowledge to their offspring. A second obstacle seemed to be parents' reluctance to be exposed as inadequate in the eyes of their children.[16]

- About 75 percent of the participants in participation training programs indicate the belief that they have been helped (a) to understand better their relationship to others and (b) to communicate better with others.[17]

- It has been recommended that experimental institutes be designed and conducted in which the Starting and Expanding Phases of the Indiana Plan are taught in two

---

[13]Jackson, Norman, An Exploratory Adult Education Program for Parents and their Children of Senior High School Age to Improve Communication in the Home, Unpublished Doctoral Thesis (Indiana University, 1964), pp. 163-164.

[14]Significant at the .05 level of confidence, Jackson, Op. Cit., p. 140. Level of confidence is an indication, by percentage, of the number of times the findings could be attributed to pure chance.

[15]Ibid., p. 163.

[16]Ibid., p. 164.

[17]Ibid., p. 162.

separate institutes instead of one. An alternative
recommendation suggested lengthening by a few days the
standard 5-day institute in order to meet the following
needs:

    (a) to allow participants more opportunities to ex-
plore and resolve interpersonal concerns that
arise during training.

    (b) to allow more time for trainers and participants
to deal with problems of transferring institute
training to local church settings.[18]

- At least three major theoretical and practical issues[19]
relevant to the task of the trainer seem to be at least
partially unresolved:

    (a) how to give sufficient attention to individual
interests, needs, and problems in situations in
which the client is the group (not the participants as individual persons).

    (b) how to achieve a creative balance between atten-
tion to group-relevant problems and inter- and
intrapersonal relationships.

    (c) how to enhance a diagnostic objectivity when the
trainer is perceived as a giver of rewards and
punishments.

- The effective trainer[20] must possess certain characteristics of personal adequacy and a constellation of
skills in the following five categories:

    (a) ability to function productively as a group member

    (b) ability to maintain a sense of personal security

    (c) ability to beget trust

    (d) ability to hold and articulate the substantive
and procedural knowledge appropriate to training

    (e) ability to exemplify the training skills he teaches

- In participation training groups the individual participant's perceptions of himself and others are probably
altered through his assuming of various service roles

_____

[18]Frye, Roye M., _The Theory of Training and the Trainer
Role in the Indiana Plan Institute_, Unpublished Doctoral Thesis
(Indiana University, 1963), pp. 149-150.

[19]_Ibid._, p. 148

[20]_Ibid._, p. 117

and the group self-appraisal process. Group self-appraisal is most effective when the identification --analysis -- generalization procedure is followed in the handling of behavioral data.[21]

- After 7 sessions of participation training in four groups totaling 60 adults averaging 25 years of age, measurable positive gains were noted in the participants' behaviors in categories described as self-confidence, self-control, responsible group participation, sociability, and trust in others. All gains were towards positive change, but the gains were not statistically significant. The investigator concluded that 7 sessions were too few to produce significant behavioral changes in the behavioral areas listed above.[22]

- After 30 contact hours of participation training (one 3-hour session each day for 10 consecutive days) in a group of 18 middle-aged adult alcoholics, significant positive changes occurred in the participants' self-concepts: in increased self-regard[23] and better adjustments to the social values[24] and environment.

- In self-report situations participants tend to rate themselves as having made more progress than is indicated by trainers and other more objective observers.[25]

- After 18 one-hour sessions of participation training conducted 3 times a week for 6 weeks, a group of 44 residents of a home for the aged (in two training groups) dwindled to 23 interested participants. The participants' average age was 79 years. No significant changes in behavior were obtained.[26]

---

[21]Ibid., p. 145.

[22]Zeller, Ernest J., A Short-term Adult Education Experiment in a Correctional Institution, Unpublished Doctoral Thesis (Indiana University, 1966), pp. 115-117.

[23]Significant at the .01 level of confidence, Shay, Earl R., Self Concept Changes Among Alcoholic Patients in Madison (Indiana) State Hospital Resulting from Participation Training in Group Discussion, Unpublished Doctoral Thesis (Indiana University, 1963), pp. 140-147.

[24]Shay, Op. Cit., pp. 143-177.

[25]Ibid., p. 178.

[26]Mason, W. D., The Effect of a Group Discussion Program in a Home for the Aged on the Behavior Patterns of the Participants, Unpublished Doctoral Thesis (Indiana University, 1964), pp. 146, 147, 181.

- After 12 two-hour sessions of participation training conducted once a week with 2 groups of 12 middle aged church laymen, significant positive[27] behavior changes occurred in the participants' feelings of self-worth, communication, acceptance, and affirmation.

- Evidence points to the fact that participation training (a) improves communication between participants, (b) brings controversy and tension into focus, where they tend to be less feared, (c) increases interest in being involved in the world, (d) brings participants into the kinds of relationships in which the group becomes a mirror in which they can view their own inner life, and (e) trains people for affirmation (responsibility).[28]

- Sessions 1 to 5 of participation training tend to have a high frustration level and are therefore less productive than later sessions.[29]

- The higher the person's level of manifest anxiety, the less positive his self-concept is likely to be. The more closed-minded the person, the less positive his self-concept is likely to be. These two findings corroborated the findings of many previous studies.[30]

- After 21 one-hour sessions of participation training conducted over a 7-week period with 30 participants between 65 and 83 years of age, the participants had significant positive changes in feelings of self-acceptance.[31]

- Participation training can help the aged person to restore interest in his ability to share his feelings and opinions with others.[32]

[27]Significant at the .05 level of confidence, Castle, John D., The Effect of Participation Training on the Self-system, Unpublished Doctoral Thesis (Indiana University, 1965), pp. 175-184.

[28]Ibid., pp. 180-182.

[29]Ibid., p. 181.

[30]Imbler, Irene I., The Effects of Participation Training on Closed-Mindedness, Anxiety, and Self-Concept, Unpublished Doctoral Thesis (Indiana University, 1967), p. 94.

[31]Significant at the .05 level of confidence, Miller, Charles E., The Utilization of an Adult Education Participation Training Progress To Meet Selected Educational Needs of Aged Persons, Unpublished Doctoral Thesis (Indiana University, 1963), pp. 104-105.

[32]Ibid., p. 106.

• Self satisfaction of aged persons can be increased during a participation training program.[33]

• After 12 sessions of participation training conducted for 1 3/4 hours twice a week for 6 weeks with 37 adult hospital employees having a median age of 42 years, no significant positive changes were reported in attitudes concerning acceptance of self and acceptance of others.[34]

D. PITFALLS OF APPLICATION

There are many combinations of reasons why some Indiana Plan programs have failed, in specific cases, to achieve expected results in local churches. Aside from instances of ineptitude on the part of some trainers, the following practices and beliefs have been noted as the most common pitfalls during the past 12 years of usage in hundreds of churches across the country:

1. Trying Short-Cuts to Participation Training in the Starting Phase. There seems to be no adequate way to eliminate the necessity of participants spending from 20 to 36 contact hours together in 10 to 15 sessions of discussion teamwork training and practice. Attempts to shorten the starting phase usually take the form of (a) having too few training sessions and/or (b) having training sessions that are abbreviated in length.

Usually it will be found that from 2 to 2 1/2 hours per session are needed for the most successful training operations, and that from 10 to 15 such sessions are required -- normally about 15 rather than 10. A hurried training session can be held in 1 1/2 to 2 hours, but from 2 to 2 1/2 hours make it possible to accomplish effectively the basic four tasks of each training session.[35]

---

[33]Ibid., p. 105.

[34]Significance was tested at the .20 level of confidence, Partin, Jennings J., A Study of Two Group Discussion Procedures for Changing Attitudes Toward Self and Others, Unpublished Doctoral Thesis (Indiana University, 1967), p. 110.

[35]For a full explanation of the four basic training events that are crucial to each session, the reader is referred to Chapter IV in Participation Training for Adult Education (Bethany Press, 1965), by Paul Bergevin and John McKinley.

A particularly harmful way of trying to reduce the length of each session is that of omitting or giving short shrift to the critique that must follow each discussion. If this shared evaluation period is omitted or de-emphasized, the trainer is giving up a major tool for building discussion teamwork. It is of utmost importance that participants talk openly and systematically about the events in their group life that affect their development as a learning group.

There is one way of reducing the length of time normally required for the Starting Phase. Instead of having one training session per week, the participants can adopt week-end training schedules and other time patterns described in Participation Training for Adult Education (pp. 14-15).

2. Failing to Conduct Clinics. During the past 12 years, most local church practitioners have chosen to ignore the week-end clinic described in Chapter III of this book. The few trainers who have used it, in developing programs in multiple churches in the same geographical region, have reported clinics to be quite valuable tools. The authors found them to be valuable and believe that other practitioners have not used them to advantage when their need was indicated.

The fact that inter-church clinics have not been widely used is an indication of how difficult it is to get us to place priority upon activities that seem not to be directly concerned with self or with a small group to which we feel strongly attached. It is most difficult for persons to think at the level of the parish and the community, which is a major purpose of the clinic program. And yet, individuals and small groups, not just parish programs, benefit from the clinic experience.

3. Using the Institute for Trainers as a Parish Program. The Institute for Trainers was not devised as a format for local church programing. It is misused when applied in the local church setting. For example, participants in the 5-day institute for trainers experience the planned expansion phase (of

local church programing) in two days in an intensive, telescoped format; normal parish program operations are abbreviated and compressed in time so that institute participants can have some experience with planned expansion programs in a short space of time. In the local church setting, several weeks are required to identify an educational need, plan a program (and learn how to plan while planning), and publicize and conduct an expanded educational program, particularly if the new program is to involve a number of parishioners in significant ways. In the local church, planning and program promotion must proceed at a natural pace. If the institute program, with its unnaturally accelerated pace, is attempted in the parish setting, relatively few regular parishioners can be expected to take advantage of it. Also many other advantages of slow, evolutionary program development are lost.

4. De-emphasizing of the Expansion Phase. Some practitioners de-emphasize the Expansion Phase of the Indiana Plan for various reasons. One way of doing this is to use only the participation training component of the Plan (see item #6, "Fear of sudden Change.")

De-emphasis of planned expansion, although a prerogative of the practitioner, is a pitfall to be avoided. Even if the local church has an existing adult program which it wishes to preserve, the Indiana Plan can be expanded in ways that will strengthen, not destroy, the established program. It is reasonable to assume, however, that to strengthen an existing program is to change it in desirable ways (that is, in ways that make it a more effective vehicle for education.) To deny this is to assume that an existing program cannot be improved upon. The following assumptions and factors seem to justify some kind of planned expansion program for a parish in which participation training is being used:

    a. Parishioners in local churches have educational problems and needs which the present program either does not deal with or does not deal with adequately. Identification of such needs and problems, and basing programs on them, are basic tasks of expansion.

b. It is desirable for an increasing number of adult parishioners to share in program development since learners tend to become more responsible for learning (1) when they are given a share in planning and (2) when they learn how to do so effectively. The expansion phase can be designed to activate these factors and attract more participants to adult programs in the church.

c. Knowledge about and experience in goal setting and evaluation, coupled with freedom of expression, are desirable assets for a maximum number of adult learners involved in the parish adult program. These conditions are promoted in the parish at large by effective expansion programs.

d. It is desirable to establish or broaden the accepting-sharing-helping relationship among a maximum number of persons in the congregational family, since this relationship assists members of the family to learn and work and worship together productively. This is a major purpose of planned expansion programs.

e. It is desirable to increase the amount and quality of interpersonal communication among parishioners on aspects of Christian living that parishioners consider significant.

In participation training, the groundwork is laid for accomplishing the long range tasks embodied in the points listed above. Expansion phase programs of various kinds that are designed to promote these tasks on a broad scale are necessary if the real potential is to be gained from participation training.

5. <u>Using Inadequate Critique Procedures</u>. Evidence from field programs indicates that several trainers in local churches do not use critique procedures effectively and systematically. Since there is some natural embarrassment among participants when they are confronted, in critiques, with lapses in their discussion teamwork, trainers sometimes avoid dealing with process factors. This failure is especially critical in early sessions when the trainer is responsible for initiating and legitimizing the group standard for dealing openly with process factors.

There is no good substitute for (1) examining the group efforts in terms of specific role responsibilities and obstructions to individual communication and learning and (2) getting the participants to discuss their perceptions regarding these factors in an effort to improve the educational activity and their role in it. This critique evaluation cannot be conducted effectively in 5 or 10 minutes and it must be given direction by the trainer for several sessions, until the standard has been established that supports open, systematic evaluation.

The tendency to let the volunteer observer define, in his observer's report given directly after the discussion, the process factors which the group will discuss in the critique is an ineffective practice. It reflects the fear and insecurity of the trainer. The volunteer observer is, himself, learning to observe process factors and thus cannot be expected to identify a sufficient number of relevant process factors. His report must usually be supplemented by a trainer-led discussion to evaluate additional process factors. Trainers are asked to read carefully pp. 60-64 in Participation Training for Adult Education for guidance on conducting critiques.

6. Fear of Sudden Change. Evidence shows that in many local churches which have well-established programs of adult education, clergymen and lay leaders avoid using the full potential of the Indiana Plan because they fear it will produce sudden changes in their already established program. This fear is particularly strong in some churches which have high financial and/or strong emotional commitments to denominational printed materials and quasi-prescribed program formats. Persons in these local church situations who use the Indiana Plan are most likely (a) to use only the participation training component and (b) to encourage the persons they train to use their new ideas by accepting leadership roles that need to be filled in the church. This adaptation of the Plan as a leadership training device is ironic, particularly when we reflect upon the fact that one of the problems which the Plan was designed to

correct was an overemphasis on leadership training at the expense of training for all learners in how to learn together. It raises the interesting educational question of the futility of having trained leaders working with learners who do not know how to make the most effective use of trained leaders to further their own learning.

Participation training as used in the Indiana Plan does not ignore the significance of well trained leadership, but it does put "leadership" in a different perspective by training all participants in the art of participation, of which leadership is one of several important roles.

The fact seems clear that people tend to bend new tools (participation training) to do old familiar tasks (leadership training) without seriously questioning the validity of the old task. New means to old ends are easier to teach than new ends. The fact is, that participation training includes leader training as well as "learner training." The fear that is generated by the idea of training all learners stems probably from the belief by some educators, that (a) their own role will in some way be threatened, and (b) learners do not need to learn how to learn together -- but only to listen.

Although the leadership training adaptation of the Indiana Plan is a legitimate one for its limited purpose, it cannot be said that the Plan has really been used in that situation, at least in a way that would lead us to expect the kind of results that could come from a well-developed program based on the Indiana Plan.

7. Unwillingness or Inability of Persons to Take the Long View of Evolutionary Program Development. The kinds of changes sought in persons and congregations (listed in #4 above) are never achieved completely or rapidly. By its very nature the Indiana Plan is a framework of training and programing that aims chiefly at developing instrumental conditions that promote effective Christian learning within persons and among persons.

Shared planning, group evaluation, freedom of expression, improved communication, acceptance, sensitivity to others' individual needs as learners, and the use of procedural skills relevant to group learning -- these are factors that require several years of effort to activate as consciously-used factors in the broad group life of a congregation of average size.

A pitfall to avoid in this respect is the expectation of startling results in a short period of time. One or two training groups cannot transform a congregation into an ideal learning society in a year's time. (They can make a startling difference in a small congregation in one year, however). Patience and unremitting effort are absolutely necessary. Those who seek to revolutionize the parish in one year by using the Indiana Plan will probably fail (unless it is a very small parish) for the following reasons:

a. The Indiana Plan requires the introduction of many new norms. These norms must be initiated and learned through experience and accepted by a maximum number of persons. This process requires time.

b. Since the church is a voluntary organization, and somewhat peripheral to many persons, many parishioners do not spend significant amounts of time together regularly throughout the week. Changing norms in a group is partly a function of being together for significant periods of time.

c. When the members of a participation training group (who have spent much time together learning) try to impose new educational ideas on the rest of the congregation they encounter resistance, which is natural.

d. Changes are most likely to be accepted when they are small changes, when they are introduced slowly rather than suddenly, and when a significant number of respected persons in the group or congregation accept the changes and encourage them. It takes time to fulfill these conditions in a group as large as a congregation.

8. Tendency to Think of Adult Education in the Church as a Peripheral Activity. One of the pitfalls of a training program such as the Indiana Plan is the tendency of some persons to exploit training groups and turn them into social action groups. The issue is not whether concerned people should become active, responsible citizens and do something about what they learn;

144

they should. But active responsible persons also need to be informed persons. An education program can help persons to continue to become mature, and, while it can serve to support persons who are engaged in social action projects, the program is not, in itself, a mechanism of social action. Those persons who would transform an educational group into a social action group are abandoning the educational enterprise, which is needed to support effective social action. Even if social action is substituted in the name of education, it is an indication that systematic learning based on mental discipline is being considered as a peripheral activity.

Others believe that the practicing Christian need only pray and worship faithfully in order to become more mature. For some persons these activities might be enough, but an overwhelming number of persons whom the authors have encountered have found vital educational programs to be of some help in their quest for Christian maturity. It is our observation that the uninformed social activist, the autocrat and the mystical zealot who places all hope for human change in some ineffable experience tend to have one attitude in common. They tend to think of adult education in the church as a peripheral experience.

These three kinds of persons seem to consider lay adult education as peripheral for perhaps different reasons. The uninformed social activist wants results right now; he seeks quick change and can't wait for the slow handmaiden of education. The autocrat thinks he already knows what the learners need and must learn; any open educational system he is not in control of threatens him and is peripheral to his real objectives; transmitting his idea of truth and satisfying a personal need to be in control.

The person who interprets all significant human change as the result of some ineffable experience beyond the mind of man is abandoning, in part, the concept of human responsibility. To him, education that emphasizes the responsibility of the learner to seek and express himself is peripheral because it

145

seems to deny God's power by holding forth the false hope that man can do something on his own about his condition by exerting his intellectual powers. These persons are usually unwilling to describe, even provisionally, specific human outcomes that should result from an effective adult program; they prefer to speak of ultimate goals only, for their eyes are fixed on a spiritual realm that is ultimate. They seek refuge in the power of faith as an exclusive educational change agent. They are essentially medieval scholastics who are painfully caught in a world that has already demonstrated the practical usefulness of human gifts combined with faith to carry on adult education for God-centered living.

A GLOSSARY OF TERMS

Acceptance: an uncensuring attitude toward a person's behavior and recognition of his worth as a person without condemning or condoning his actions or expressions.

Adult: a person who has reached physical maturity.

Adult Education: (a) the process through which adults use opportunities to learn systematically under the guidance of an agency, teacher, or leader; (b) experiences in day-to-day living which cause adult behavioral change; (c) the study of the professional field of adult education.

Attitude: a state of mental and emotional readiness to react to situations, persons, or things in a manner in harmony with an habitual pattern of response.

Authoritarian: a person who advocates the principle of obedience to authority as opposed to individual liberty or self-direction.

Authority: an accepted source of information, direction, or guidance.

Clinic: an extended series of meetings that involves diagnosis, analysis and treatment of conditions or problems.

Co-leader: a participant whose primary responsibility is to help the discussion leader to coordinate the discussion.

Communication: a sharing of ideas, thoughts, and feelings between and among persons.

Consensus: a tentative working agreement which is usually the result of concessions made when the majority and the minority views are evaluated and taken into consideration.

Consolidating Phase: the third phase of program development in the Indiana Plan, in which all trained persons seek to establish the training program as a stable, continuing series of activities adapted to the needs of the local church.

Content: mainly the substantive information (subject matter) in a learning program. The "what" of education as compared with the "how." The "what" could be considered content, the "how," process.

Creative Learning: an educational process in which the learners themselves make discoveries that are new to them and that lead toward desirable growth.

147

Critique: a portion of a meeting in which the participants analyze (as objectively as possible) the strengths and weaknesses of their educational activity.

Discussion Leader: a participant whose primary responsibility is to help the group participants work together effectively toward achievement of group goals.

Evaluation: judging the effectiveness of an adult education experience in terms of the goals.

Expanding Phase: the second training phase of the Indiana Plan, in which participants broaden their skills and impact through a variety of planned educational activities designed to involve more persons and to improve the potential of parish life.

Freedom of Expression: the absence of undue restraint in telling others our thoughts and feelings

Goal: a desired result or outcome which participants hope to achieve.

Group Discussion: a purposeful, cooperative exploration qf a topic of mutual interest by six to twenty persons under the guidance of a trained leader.

Group Participants: the persons who discuss the topic and for whose benefit the discussion exists; all other participants perform service roles to help the group participants.

Institute: an extended series of meetings which provide specific and authoritative instruction by qualified specialists.

Interest: something a learner would like to learn about or come to understand better. Used as a basis to identify needs which can be treated educationally.

Need (felt): something regarded as necessary by the person concerned.

Need (real educational): specific understandings, feelings, attitudes, and/or skills that are (a) lacking, (b) required for the client to attain a more desirable condition based on some system of values, and (c) attainable through educational activities.

Need (symptomatic educational): a manifestation of a need which a person considers real; could be used as a clue to a real need.

Observer: a participant whose major responsibility is to observe how the group functions and to report his observations when called upon -- usually in the critique period.

Outward Growth: a term used to describe the basic dynamic of an effective program as one which encourages (a) application of new knowledge, (b) reversal of the trend toward extreme self-centeredness, and (c) movement toward socio-centeredness.

Participant: a person who takes part in the training program by assuming one of these roles: trainer, discussion leader, group participant, observer, resource person, or co-leader. All of these participants working together toward common goals would be considered a learning team.

Participation Training: in this book, a program designed to help participants learn how to use the processes and procedures of group discussion more effectively. Also a system of education which can help people to "learn how to learn."

Problem (educational): a condition or obstacle that learners can overcome through educational activities; can be considered as specific human difficulties of perceiving, thinking, understanding, feeling, and acting.

Procedure: a systematic series of actions designed to accomplish a task.

Process: the flow of all the intra- and inter-personal factors involved in how persons communicate and learn as opposed to what they communicate and learn (content).

Resource Person: a person who has had special training and/or significant experience in the subject that is discussed and who serves the group by furnishing authoritative information when called upon.

Starting Phase: the initial training phase of the Indiana Plan, in which participants learn how to learn together through the development of discussion teamwork.

Task: a job to be done; an instrumental activity that leads to the achieving of a goal.

Trainer: the participant who is trained to help all other participants understand and use group processes and procedures more effectively.

AN ANNOTATED BIBLIOGRAPHY OF WRITINGS ABOUT THE INDIANA PLAN

The following items comprise a selected bibliography of writings about the Indiana Plan considered by the authors to be significant. They include doctoral degree dissertations written by investigators who have studied topics related directly to the plan or some aspect of it and articles by persons who report on (a) their use of the plan in local churches and other situations, and (b) their reactions to the institute for trainers.

1. *The Acts and Proceedings of the Ninety-Fourth General Assembly of the Presbyterian Church in Canada*, Toronto, Ontario, June 5-12, 1968. Thorn Press, Toronto, p. 304.

In this annual report, the General Assembly acknowledges that several persons in several synods had had training and positive experiences with the Indiana Plan; the board strongly commends the plan to synod and presbytery committees and offers assistance in securing trained personnel and in holding institutes.

2. Barringer, Kenneth D., "Religious Education for Adults," *Adult Leadership*, XVII, No. 1 (May, 1968), p. 12.

An account of how the United Methodist Church has sought to introduce a new approach to curriculum for adults; mentions the Indiana Plan as one of a few programs that "offer tremendous possibilities for intensive training ventures for local church leaders."

3. Bergevin, Paul, *A Philosophy for Adult Education* (Seabury Press, 1967), 177 pp.

Describes basic concepts and principles which undergird the development of effective adult education programs in a free society; supports the idea of program development exemplified in the Indiana Plan.

4. Boyd, Lois Rogers, "Adult Education in Action: Reports on the use of the Indiana Plan in a Local Church," *The Bethany Guide*, XXXII, No. 11 (August, 1958), pp. 30-31.

Written by a lay woman who reports on using the plan with 25 adults over an 8-month period; includes outcomes as perceived by the trainer and the other participants.

5. Castle, John D., <u>The</u> <u>Effect</u> <u>of</u> <u>Participation</u> <u>Train-</u><u>ing</u> <u>on</u> <u>the</u> <u>Self-System</u>, Unpublished doctoral thesis (Indiana University, 1965), 216 pp.

An experimental study, involving 24 church laymen, of the extent to which participation training can lead to significant behavioral changes in the "self-system" in the areas of self-worth, communication, acceptance, and affirmation.

6. Chappell, Carl, "Participation Training: An Instrument for Milieu Change," <u>Hospital</u> <u>and</u> <u>Community</u> <u>Psychiatry</u>, XX, No. 11 (Nov., 1969), pp. 355-357.

An in-service training director in a mental hospital describes how he has used participation training to promote milieu therapy through training programs for hospital employees; briefly describes outcomes of the program.

7. Croft, The Very Rev. Fred, "The Indiana Plan," <u>The</u> <u>Living</u> <u>Church</u>, CXL, No. 22 (May 29, 1960), pp. 14-15.

Describes the reaction of an institute participant and constitutes his attempt to describe the Indiana Plan in his own words to persons in his denomination.

8. Devik, The Very Rev. Rudolph, "Successful Formula for Adult Education," <u>Christian</u> <u>Education</u> <u>Findings</u>, VII, No. 1 (January, 1959), Seabury Press, pp. 18-19.

Written by the Canon Missioner of the Episcopal Diocese of Olympia, this article reports on the results of adapting the Indiana Plan to different situations after training 60 laity and clergy.

9. Dollins, Curtis N., <u>The</u> <u>Effect</u> <u>of</u> <u>Group</u> <u>Discussion</u> <u>as</u> <u>a</u> <u>Learning</u> <u>Procedure</u> <u>on</u> <u>the</u> <u>Adaptive</u> <u>Social</u> <u>Behavior</u> <u>of</u> <u>Educable</u> <u>Adult</u> <u>Mental</u> <u>Retardates</u>, Unpublished doctoral thesis (Indiana University, 1967) 191 pp.

A study involving the experimental application of participation training, in a discussion program for 35 educable adult retardates, for the purpose of determining the extent to which desirable changes in adaptive social behavior could be encouraged.

10. Drane, Richard S., <u>The</u> <u>Effects</u> <u>of</u> <u>Participation</u> <u>Train-</u><u>ing</u> <u>on</u> <u>Adult</u> <u>Literacy</u> <u>Education</u> <u>in</u> <u>a</u> <u>Mental</u> <u>Hospital</u>, Unpublished doctoral thesis (Indiana University, 1967), 114 pp.

A study to determine whether participation training followed by literacy instruction would be more effective than literacy instruction alone.

11. Ehrlich, Theodore J., "An Experimental College Work Program," _Religious Education_, LV, No. 2 (March-April, 1960), pp. 94-98.

Reports on the effect of an adaptation of the Indiana Plan on the campus religious work of St. Stephens' Episcopal Church at Indiana State University.

12. Ernsberger, David J., _A Philosophy of Adult Christian Education_, The Westminister Press (Philadelphia, 1959), pp. 139-141.

An attack on the Indiana Plan by a writer who had had no training in or experience with the Plan; charges that the Plan virtually ignores the problem of relating participation to content. Sample of criticism: "The emphasis on group dynamics techniques in the Indiana Plan seems to result in such a preoccupation with subjective reactions to the content that the group will never get around to exploring the content itself."

13. Frye, Roye M., _The Theory of Training and the Trainer Role in the Indiana Plan Institute_, Unpublished doctoral thesis (Indiana University, 1963), 186 pp.

An analysis of the educational theory which is implicit in the Indiana Plan Institute and an investigation of the trainer role as the focal means of guiding the participants' experience.

14. Geisert, Mollie M., _The Study of Two Heterogeneous Educational-level Groups in a Participation Training Program of Adult Education: An Experiment in a Mental Hospital_, Unpublished doctoral thesis (Indiana University, 1965), 233 pp.

Investigates the relationship of educational level of participants (schizophrenic patients) to their changes in willingness and ability to communicate and to help others through participation training.

15. Gordon, George K., _A Q-Sort Instrument for Measuring Attitudes Toward the Educational Conditions of the Indiana Plan_, Unpublished doctoral thesis (Indiana University, 1965), 203 pp.

A developmental study in which the author designed, validated, and tested an instrument to measure attitude changes of participants toward the educational conditions of the Indiana Plan during the course of an institute.

16. Groves, Joe, "The Indiana Plan," _Resource_, Vol. VI, No. 7, (April, 1965), pp. 18-19.

Written by a layman in the Lutheran Church of America who describes how the Indiana Plan was gradually introduced in the church; describes considerable impact made on his small urban church, with noted improvements in the Sunday School, committee meetings, and council meetings.

17. Hazen, Robert, "Adult Education: We Learned It as We Lived It," Christian Leadership, XM, No. 7, (July, 1959), pp. 10-11.

Describes the experience and reactions of 19 ministers of the Church of God, (Anderson, Indiana), in an Indiana Plan institute from the viewpoint of one of the participants.

18. Imbler, Irene I., The Effects of Participation Training on Closed-Mindedness, Anxiety, and Self-Concept, Unpublished doctoral thesis (Indiana University, 1967), 126 pp.

An experimental study of the extent to which a participation training program can reduce closed-mindedness and anxiety and improve self-concept; participants were 25 labor leaders in a residential labor education program.

19. Jackson, Norman W., An Exploratory Adult Education for Parents and their Children of Senior High Age to Improve Communication in the Home, Unpublished doctoral thesis, (Indiana University, 1964), 188 pp.

A study of the effects of participation training on 35 adults and 18 teenagers who took part in participation training groups organized according to three different program patterns.

20. Kamitsuka, Arthur J., A Conceptual Scheme for an Adaptation of Participation Training in Adult Education for use in the Three Love Movement in Japan, Unpublished doctoral thesis (Indiana University, 1969), 299 pp.

Describes a conceptual scheme for adapting participation training to provide participants in the Three Love Movement with opportunities to learn and practice democratic ideas and practices.

21. Mason, Wendel Dean, The Effect of a Group Discussion Program in a Home for the Aged on the Behavior Patterns of the Participants, Unpublished doctoral thesis (Indiana University, 1969), 242 pp.

An experimental study in which guiding principles of the Indiana Plan were activated in a home for the aged in an attempt to increase selected positive behaviors.

22. McKinley, John, A Participation Training Program in a Mental Hospital: An Experiment in Adult Education, Unpublished doctoral thesis (Indiana University, 1960), 271 pp.

A study of the application of participation training to 22 hospitalized adult schizophrenic patients between 60 and 82 years of age.

23. Miller, Charles E., _The Utilization of an Adult Educa-
     tion Program of Group Discussion with Participation
     Training to Meet Selected Needs of Aged Persons_, Un-
     published doctoral thesis (Indiana University, 1963),
     133 pp.

Describes experimental application of a 21-session participation training program to 30 persons between 65 and 83 years
of age in a home for the aged.

24. Partin, James J., _A Study of Two Group Discussion Pro-
     cedures for Changing Attitudes Toward Acceptance of
     Self and Others_, Unpublished doctoral thesis (Indiana
     University, 1967), 145 pp.

A study of two adaptations of participation training applied
experimentally to 37 attendants at a state hospital in an effort
to determine the extent to which acceptance of self and others
could be increased.

25. Peel, Donald N., _The Philosophy of Adult Education of
     the Anglican Church of Canada_, Unpublished doctoral
     thesis (Indiana University, 1967), 553 pp.

A critical analysis of the nature of the philosophy of
adult education in the Anglican Church of Canada; the author
comments (pp. 491-95) on the nature of the Indiana Plan and why
it can be adapted to the educational problems of that church.

26. Senturk, Celal, _Analysis of Selected Characteristics
     of Adult Education Institute Participants_, Unpublished
     master's thesis (Indiana University, 1966), 48 pp.

A study of the characteristics of persons who participated
in institutes for trainers in the Indiana Plan between the years
1959-1965.

27. Shay, Earl R., _Self-Concept Changes Among Alcoholic
     Patients in Madison State Hospital Resulting from Par-
     ticipation Training in Group Discussion_, Unpublished
     doctoral thesis (Indiana University, 1963), 206 pp.

A study of the experimental application of participation
training with 18 male alcoholic patients; an attempt to ascer-
tain resulting changes in self-concepts.

28. Smith, Robert M., "One Hundred and Fifty Institutes in
     Adult Education," _Adult Leadership_, XIV, No. 3 (Septem-
     ber, 1965), pp. 90-91.

Summarizes the tasks and goals of the Indiana Plan institutes up to 1965; written by a certified staff trainer who also
appraises its use in the light of its 10 years of operation.

29. Smith, Robert M., "Some Uses of Participation Training," Adult Leadership, XVIII, No. 3 (September, 1969), pp. 77-78, 96.

Written by a certified staff trainer in the Indiana Plan, this article compares participation training and sensitivity training as to procedures and characteristics; lists unique advantages of each; describes how the author adapted the Indiana Plan, in the Detroit area, to the training of more than 800 persons involved in O.E.O. and other programs; describes rather dramatic positive results in various areas.

30. Steffer, Robert Wesley, A Study of Delayed Achievement in a Short-Term Adult Education Program, Unpublished doctoral thesis (Indiana University, 1967), 155 pp.

Describes the effectiveness of a 5-session program of participation training in group discussion with 24 persons in a local church one year later.

31. Stenson, Stanford O., The Development of Listening Skills Through the Indiana Plan Institute and Integrated Training Programs, Unpublished doctoral thesis (Indiana University, 1969), 196 pp.

A study of the extent to which the Indiana Plan institute develops listening skills and the effects of including an experimental listening training component as part of the institute training program.

STUDIES IN PROGRESS

1. Harshman, Eugene, The Augmentation of Attitude Change in Participation Training: A Trainer Model Derived from the Rogerian Therapist Role, Doctoral thesis in progress (Indiana University).

An investigation of elements of trainer role behaviors relevant to both participation training and Rogerian therapy.

2. Connelly, H. Walton, An Investigation of the Effects of Microlabs and Instrumented Exercises on Desired Behavioral Outcomes in Participation Training, Doctoral thesis in progress (Indiana University).

A study of the effects of using microlabs and instrumented exercises as part of the training format of a 3-day institute in participation training.

3. Coles, Laurence W., (Title undecided), Doctoral thesis in progress (Indiana University).

A study designed to evaluate and compare the effects of member-trained and leader-trained types of leadership on Methodist adult groups; the member-trained type of leadership is based on the training program of the Indiana Plan; involves 35 churches in the mid-West.

4. Tiley, Arden, (untitled), Title III Project, Resource Center, Highland Park School, Detroit, Michigan.

A curriculum specialist is experimenting with the application of participation training with groups of 9th and 11th grade students in the public school.

Acceptance: importance of, 36; nature of, 52; significance of in the learning process, 57; and identification, 47; definition of, 147.

Adult: nature of as learner, 2-9; as dependent and independent, 61; ego-centered nature of, 81-83; definition of, 147; capacity of as a learner, 67-68.

Adult Education: in the church, ii, iii; see also, Church, adult learning in, and Religious education, adult.

Aggression: 50.

Ambivalence: 57.

Anger: 47, 114.

Association: value of, 81.

Attendance: interest factors in, 64-66; 73-74; records of, 74.

Authoritariansim: 36, 59; definition of, 147.

Authority: and dependency, 41-42; and rebellion, 42.

Bible: and standardized programs, 16, 76; and the Indiana Plan, 76.

Catharsis: as release, 28.

Church: educational goal of, 1; non-productive adult learning in, 2-19; forces now affecting it as an institution, 125-131; the ecumenical movement in, and the Indiana Plan, 125-126; adult education considered as a peripheral activity in, 144-146.

Change: 49; fear of, and the Indiana Plan, 142 ff.

Clinic: in the Indiana Plan, 102-103, 107, 147; failure to conduct, 139.

Communication: nature and definition of, 31; and creative self-expression, 110; evidence of personal growth in, 116-117.

Community: Church and, 80.

Competition: and cooperation, 115.

Conflict: adjusting to, 47-48, 50; resolution of in learning, 57; presence of in learning situation, 113.

Content: and process, 16-17; and process in self-examination, 84; definition of, 147; see also, Subject matter and Process.

Cooperation: and unity, 39; and ambivalence, 57; criteria of, 112 ff.

Creative learning: 57; and freedom of expression, 35-36; definition of, 147.

Critique: inadequate use of, 141-142; definition of, 148.

Democracy: meaning of, 36.

Disagreement: and maturity, 114, 115.

Discipline: misunderstanding of, 38; see Self-discipline.

Education: system of, in transition, 58 ff.; formal characteristics of, 77-78; informal characteristics of, 78-79.

Egoism: 82; see also Adult, as learner, ego-centered nature of.

Equality: 67.

Evaluation: avoidance of and obstacles to, 13-15; in the Indiana Plan, 103-104; definition of, 148; see also Critique.

Expansion phase: of the Indiana Plan, description of, 93-100; de-emphasis of as a pitfall, 140-141; see also Expanding phase; definition of, 148.

Fear: 7-9; 40, 41, 72.

Feelings: 16-17, 53-54, 56; articulation of, 43-44.

Force: 68.

Free choice: 70.

Freedom: limitations of, 29, 38.

Freedom of expression: definition of, 27; use as an educational condition,